Linux Enterprise Sci-Fi

Scripts & Archivos de Configurado

ESTEBAN HERRERA

Editorial lescifi

ISBN: 1507869746
ISBN-13: 978-1507869741

DEDICATORIA

Al Creador y a mi familia, por permitirme sacrificar parte del tiempo que era para ustedes en este proyecto y por creer en mí.

CONTENIDOS

AGRADECIMIENTO

A toda la Comunidad Linux que de una u otra forma ha contribuido con este proyecto, a los usuarios de Linux que vieron mis videos o respondieron mis preguntas en el chat, especialmente en el IRC #dovecot, o postearon en sus webs y blogs alguna pieza que me faltaba en el rompecabezas, a los creadores y desarrolladores de Linux y Debian GNU/Linux y a los desarrolladores de aplicaciones de código abierto, a las editoriales y a los autores que publicaron los libros y revistas que más consulté y a los compañeros de trabajo que realmente me aportaron cuando lo necesité. Sin ustedes este proyecto hubiera sido imposible.

1 DESCRIPCION DE CONTENIDOS

El presente manuscrito consiste en la versión final de cada Script y Archivo de Configurado del proyecto Linux Enterprise Sci-Fi que se ha realizado completamente en video.

Todas las respuestas a preguntas que pueda tener acerca del proyecto Linux Enterprise Sci-Fi se encuentran en formato de video, en el DVD "LE SF 0: Introducción", uno de los 6 DVDs que acompañan este libro. Se debe consultar el último capítulo del libro para poder descargar el DVD sin necesidad de pagos adicionales al costo del libro. Existe una versión web oficial de la descripción del proyecto en YouTube, en el canal "lescifi", que incluye los siguientes videos:

Objetivos del proyecto Linux Enterprise Sci-Fi
Objetivos del proyecto 2
Hacia quién va dirigido LE Sci-Fi?
Lo que LE Sci-Fi no contiene
Contenidos de Linux Enterprise Sci-Fi
Caducidad del proyecto
Calidad de audio
Linux Enterprise Sci-Fi en YouTube
Listas de reproducción en YouTube
Formato de video y requerimientos del sistema
Pasos de instalación para iniciar tu proyecto
Por qué preferir GNU/Linux?
Ejemplo 1 – Virtualización en progreso
Migración a VMware® Workstation

Para acceder directamente a la lista de reproducción del canal tenemos disponible la siguiente dirección:
https://www.youtube.com/playlist?list=PLAUbu6yaxZnr-phZuP8bYF_A42YgQz06e

Los DVDs descargables además contienen toda la documentación necesaria para comprender los archivos y el proyecto y desarrollarlo por su propia cuenta como si de un curso de guitarra en video se tratara. Estas imágenes ISO incluyen los diagramas, las fotografías y presentaciones y otros documentos que han sido excluidos del manuscrito y no se incluyen en el precio de este libro, sino que se entregan para descargar como un valor agregado adicional.

Todos los archivos que se incluyen (y los que no) han sido explicados en el desarrollo de Linux Enterprise Sci-Fi en video por lo que no se han agregado notas adicionales de instalación ni configuración a los textos originales.

Hay algunos archivos que se deben crear manualmente algunas veces y no se han listado intencionalmente por no poseer contenido inicial como lo es uno del servidor de correo que va dentro del directorio /var/vmail/, /etc/balance/pass que contiene una contraseña de root y apache.log.

En vista de que la segunda parte del proyecto de Linux Enterprise Sci-Fi consiste en la construcción de ambientes de clusters o granjas de servidores de uso general con Linux a partir de un servidor de tipo stand-alone y bastión previamente diseñado en una primera parte, existirán archivos donde se debe cambiar una o más opciones para poder replicarlo en cada uno de los hosts configurados en máxima disponibilidad (HA), por lo que hemos decidido utilizar un único nombre de host ¨x2¨ que cuando aparezca se interprete como uno entre varios hosts que se deben preparar para que trabajen en conjunto, sincronizadamente. Todos los hosts utilizados en el proyecto se configuran en pantalla en cada video programa para evitar así confusiones y errores potenciales relacionados con su multiplicidad, es decir que podrá utilizar los archivos aquí descritos algunas veces como versiones finales y otras veces como plantillas. Recuerde hacer copias de respaldo de todas las versiones originales de los archivos que modifica en el sistema antes de proceder a realizarles cambios.

El objetivo primordial de este libro es facilitar y acelerar el proceso de re-creación de la infraestructura de Linux Enterprise Sci-Fi en cualquier tipo de ambiente de su empresa, laboratorio u ordenador, manteniendo todo el texto necesario impreso secuencialmente por fuera de la pantalla del monitor en que se encuentre estudiando los video programas, a modo de guía de bolsillo.

Por último, debo aclarar que todas las marcas y nombres de programas mencionados en los Archivos de Configurado así como en los Scripts ejecutables y en muchos casos los propios archivos son registrados y/o propiedad intelectual de sus respectivos dueños o representantes u organizaciones y no se está intentando obtener ningún beneficio económico ni perjudicarlos con el hecho de que sean mencionados o expuestos en este libro.

2 ARCHIVOS DE CONFIGURADO

Host: vgui.

Función: Cliente gráfico Virtual Machine Manager para la virtualización de KVM, VMware®, etc. Monitor de recursos de infraestructura de red, DMZ y granja de servidores en cluster de máxima disponibilidad (HA).

Archivos modificados o creados:

En el sistema:

```
/* -----------------
      /etc/hosts
------------------ */
127.0.0.1     localhost
127.0.1.1     vgui.aestudio.sytes.net vgui

#192.168.1.198   foobar.aestudio.sytes.net foobar
192.168.1.199   foobar.aestudio.sytes.net foobar

192.168.1.200   x1.aestudio.sytes.net x1 mx1 mail1
192.168.1.201   x1.aestudio.sytes.net x1 mx1 mail1
192.168.1.202   x1.aestudio.sytes.net x1 mx1 mail1
192.168.1.203   x1.aestudio.sytes.net x1 mx1 mail1
192.168.1.204   x1.aestudio.sytes.net x1 mx1 mail1
192.168.1.205   x2.aestudio.sytes.net x2 mx2 mail2
192.168.1.206   x2.aestudio.sytes.net x2 mx2 mail2
192.168.1.207   x2.aestudio.sytes.net x2 mx2 mail2
192.168.1.208   x2.aestudio.sytes.net x2 mx2 mail2
192.168.1.209   x2.aestudio.sytes.net x2 mx2 mail2

# The following lines are desirable for IPv6 capable hosts
```

```
::1     ip6-localhost ip6-loopback
fe00::0 ip6-localnet
ff00::0 ip6-mcastprefix
ff02::1 ip6-allnodes
ff02::2 ip6-allrouters
```

El resto de los archivos de configurado de este host no han sido modificados desde la terminal ni se han diseñado scripts ejecutables personalizados para el mismo, ya que se ha diseñado como host de prueba. Tampoco se le ha diseñado un firewall. Sin embargo, deben existir en el host como mínimo los siguientes archivos creados o modificados por el sistema o mediante comandos o programas utilizados:

En el sistema:

/etc/hostname
/etc/network/interfaces
/etc/apt/sources.list

En el espacio de root:

/root/.ssh/known_hosts

En el espacio de usuario xcapncrunchx:

/home/xcapncrunchx/.ssh/id_dsa
/home/xcapncrunchx/.ssh/id_dsa.pub
/home/xcapncrunchx/.ssh/known_hosts

Host: xClient.

Función: Máquina cliente remoto y local corriendo Linux en modo gráfico. Usada para probar el correo electrónico certificado y todos los servicios Web disponibles.

Archivos modificados o creados:

En el sistema:

```
/* ----------------
    /etc/hosts
------------------ */
127.0.0.1     localhost
127.0.1.1     xclient.aestudio.sytes.net xclient

#192.168.1.198  foobar.aestudio.sytes.net foobar
192.168.1.199  foobar.aestudio.sytes.net foobar

192.168.1.200  x1.aestudio.sytes.net x1 mx1 mail1
192.168.1.201  x1.aestudio.sytes.net x1 mx1 mail1
192.168.1.202  x1.aestudio.sytes.net x1 mx1 mail1
192.168.1.203  x1.aestudio.sytes.net x1 mx1 mail1
192.168.1.204  x1.aestudio.sytes.net x1 mx1 mail1
```

```
192.168.1.205   x2.aestudio.sytes.net x2 mx2 mail2
192.168.1.206   x2.aestudio.sytes.net x2 mx2 mail2
192.168.1.207   x2.aestudio.sytes.net x2 mx2 mail2
192.168.1.208   x2.aestudio.sytes.net x2 mx2 mail2
192.168.1.209   x2.aestudio.sytes.net x2 mx2 mail2

# The following lines are desirable for IPv6 capable hosts
::1      ip6-localhost ip6-loopback
fe00::0 ip6-localnet
ff00::0 ip6-mcastprefix
ff02::1 ip6-allnodes
ff02::2 ip6-allrouters
```

El resto de los archivos de configurado de este host no han sido modificados desde la terminal ni se han diseñado scripts ejecutables personalizados para el mismo, ya que se ha diseñado como host de prueba. Tampoco se le ha diseñado un firewall. Sin embargo deben existir en el host como mínimo los siguientes archivos creados o modificados por el sistema o mediante comandos o programas utilizados:

En el sistema:

/etc/hostname
/etc/network/interfaces
/etc/apt/sources.list

En el espacio de root:

/home/xcapncrunchx/.ssh/known_hosts

En el espacio de usuario xcapncrunchx:

/home/xcapncrunchx/.ssh/known_hosts

Host: foobar.
Función: Servidor de virtualización VMware®, KVM o similares. Load balancer y proxy.
Archivos modificados o creados:
En el sistema:

```
/* ----------------
    /etc/hosts
----------------- */
127.0.0.1      localhost
127.0.1.1      foobar.aestudio.sytes.net foobar

#192.168.1.198  foobar.aestudio.sytes.net foobar
192.168.1.199  foobar.aestudio.sytes.net foobar

192.168.1.200  x1.aestudio.sytes.net x1 mx1 mail1
```

```
192.168.1.201   x1.aestudio.sytes.net x1 mx1 mail1
192.168.1.202   x1.aestudio.sytes.net x1 mx1 mail1
192.168.1.203   x1.aestudio.sytes.net x1 mx1 mail1
192.168.1.204   x1.aestudio.sytes.net x1 mx1 mail1
192.168.1.205   x2.aestudio.sytes.net x2 mx2 mail2
192.168.1.206   x2.aestudio.sytes.net x2 mx2 mail2
192.168.1.207   x2.aestudio.sytes.net x2 mx2 mail2
192.168.1.208   x2.aestudio.sytes.net x2 mx2 mail2
192.168.1.209   x2.aestudio.sytes.net x2 mx2 mail2


# The following lines are desirable for IPv6 capable hosts
::1     ip6-localhost ip6-loopback
fe00::0 ip6-localnet
ff00::0 ip6-mcastprefix
ff02::1 ip6-allnodes
ff02::2 ip6-allrouters


/* ----------------------------
        /etc/fail2ban/jail.conf
------------------------------ */
```
        Nota: Solo se incluye la sección de SSH del archivo en este libro.
```
[ssh]

enabled = true
port    = ssh
filter  = sshd
logpath = /var/log/auth.log
maxretry = 6


# Generic filter for pam. Has to be used with action which bans all ports
# such as iptables-allports, shorewall
[pam-generic]

enabled = false
# pam-generic filter can be customized to monitor specific subset of 'tty's
filter  = pam-generic
# port actually must be irrelevant but lets leave it all for some possible uses
port = all
banaction = iptables-allports
port    = anyport
logpath = /var/log/auth.log
maxretry = 6
```

```
/* ---------------------------------
        /etc/fail2ban/fail2ban.conf
---------------------------------- */
# Fail2Ban configuration file
#
# Author: Cyril Jaquier
#
# $Revision: 629 $
#

[Definition]

# Option:  loglevel
# Notes.:  Set the log level output.
#        1 = ERROR
#        2 = WARN
#        3 = INFO
#        4 = DEBUG
# Values: NUM  Default:  3
#
loglevel = 3


# Option: logtarget
# Notes.:  Set the log target. This could be a file, SYSLOG, STDERR or
STDOUT.
#        Only one log target can be specified.
#    Values:      STDOUT   STDERR   SYSLOG   file      Default:
/var/log/fail2ban.log
#
logtarget = /var/log/fail2ban.log


# Option: socket
# Notes.: Set the socket file. This is used to communicate with the daemon.
Do
#        not remove this file when Fail2ban runs. It will not be possible to
#        communicate with the server afterwards.
# Values: FILE  Default:  /var/run/fail2ban/fail2ban.sock
#
socket = /var/run/fail2ban/fail2ban.sock


/* ----------------
        /etc/fstab
----------------- */
```

```
# /etc/fstab: static file system information.
#
# Use 'blkid' to print the universally unique identifier for a
# device; this may be used with UUID= as a more robust way to name
devices
# that works even if disks are added and removed. See fstab(5).
#
# <file system> <mount point>   <type> <options>        <dump>
<pass>
proc        /proc        proc   defaults    0    0
# / was on /dev/sda1 during installation
UUID=f3864994-fc1d-49fa-a689-167dce2c5bbc  /              ext3
errors=remount-ro 0     1
# swap was on /dev/sda5 during installation
UUID=77f3a371-705a-4123-94d8-d50b67fec882 none        swap     sw
0     0
/dev/scd0      /media/cdrom0   udf,iso9660 user,noauto   0    0

# Databank:
/dev/sdb1 /mnt/databank1 ext3 rw,user,auto,umask=000 0
/dev/sdc1 /mnt/databank2 ext3 rw,user,auto,umask=000 0
/dev/sdd1 /mnt/databank3 vfat rw,user,auto,umask=000 0
```

```
/* --------------------------
     /etc/grub.d/00_header
--------------------------- */
```
Insert at the end of the file:

```
cat << EOF
set superusers="root"
password root PASSWORD_HERE
password xcapncrunchx PASSWORD_HERE
EOF
```

El resto de los cambios en todos los archivos del directorio /etc/grub.d/ para la versión 2 del gestor de arranque (Grub2) se ejecutan con el comando sed y se debe ver los videos del cartridge "9. Grub2 en host foobar con Squeeze. Aplica para host aestudio actualizado a Squeeze", del DVD "LE SF 2: Actualizaciones", para poder definir una contraseña para la pantalla de arranque del SO Linux. Alternativamente se puede buscar en Internet, en google "configurar el password de grub2 con sed" y le aseguro que allí aparecerá toda la información. De todos modos aquí les dejo el comando para que puedan hacerlo más rápido.

Para el usuario root:

$ sudo sed -i -e '/^menuentry /s/ {/ –users root {/' /etc/grub.d/10_linux /etc/grub.d/10_linux /etc/grub.d/30_os-prober /etc/grub.d/40_custom

El de un usuario como xcapncrunchx:

$ sudo sed -i -e '/^menuentry /s/ {/ –users xcapncrunchx {/' /etc/grub.d/10_linux /etc/grub.d/10_linux /etc/grub.d/30_os-prober /etc/grub.d/40_custom

Si se te olvidó hacer un backup de los archivos a modificar antes de hacer los cambios aún puedes deshacerlos con el comando:

$ sudo sed -i -e '/^menuentry /s/ –users superusuario[/B] {/ {/' /etc/grub.d/10_linux /etc/grub.d/20_memtest86+ /etc/grub.d/30_os-prober /etc/grub.d/40_custom

Todos los argumentos deben existir para que el comando funcione, incluyendo usuarios y archivos. Recordar que se debe tener siempre cuidado con el tipo de comillas que se deben usar en todo archivo y comandos (que son "", " y ``).

Para configurar la versión 1 de Grub ver la sección de "Archivos de Configurado" del host x2 en este libro.

```
/* ----------------------------
      /etc/network/interfaces
---------------------------- */
```

This file describes the network interfaces available on your system
and how to activate them. For more information, see interfaces(5).

The loopback network interface
auto lo
iface lo inet loopback

The primary network interface
allow-hotplug eth0
#iface eth0 inet dhcp
iface eth0 inet manual
        address 192.168.1.198
        netmask 255.255.255.0
        broadcast 192.168.1.255
        gateway 192.168.1.1
        # dns-* options are implemented by resolvconf
        # package, if installed
        #dns-nameservers 193.168.1.1
        #dns-search sytes.net

```
# Next is the creation of the bridge interface
auto br0
iface br0 inet static
      address 192.168.1.199
      netmask 255.255.255.0
      broadcast 192.168.1.255
      gateway 192.168.1.1
      # dns-* options are implemented by resolvconf
      # package, if installed
      #dns-nameservers 193.168.1.1
      #dns-search sytes.net

      pre-up /usr/sbin/tunctl -u xcapncrunchx -t tap0
      pre-up ifconfig tap0 up
      bridge_ports all tap0
      #bridge_ports eth0 eth1 eth2 eth3
      bridge_maxwait 0
      post-down ifconfig tap0
      post-down tunctl -d tap0


/* ------------------------
      /etc/ssh/sshd_config
------------------------- */
# Package generated configuration file
# See the sshd_config(5) manpage for details

# What ports, IPs and protocols we listen for
Port 22
# Use these options to restrict which interfaces/protocols sshd will bind to
#ListenAddress ::
#ListenAddress 0.0.0.0
Protocol 2
# HostKeys for protocol version 2
HostKey /etc/ssh/ssh_host_rsa_key
HostKey /etc/ssh/ssh_host_dsa_key
#Privilege Separation is turned on for security
UsePrivilegeSeparation yes

# Lifetime and size of ephemeral version 1 server key
KeyRegenerationInterval 3600
ServerKeyBits 768

# Logging
```

```
SyslogFacility AUTH
LogLevel INFO

# Authentication:
LoginGraceTime 120
PermitRootLogin yes
StrictModes yes

RSAAuthentication yes
PubkeyAuthentication yes
AuthorizedKeysFile      %h/.ssh/authorized_keys

# Don't read the user's ~/.rhosts and ~/.shosts files
IgnoreRhosts yes
# For this to work you will also need host keys in /etc/ssh_known_hosts
RhostsRSAAuthentication no
# similar for protocol version 2
HostbasedAuthentication no
# Uncomment if you don't trust ~/.ssh/known_hosts for
RhostsRSAAuthentication
#IgnoreUserKnownHosts yes

# To enable empty passwords, change to yes (NOT RECOMMENDED)
PermitEmptyPasswords no

# Change to yes to enable challenge-response passwords (beware issues with
# some PAM modules and threads)
ChallengeResponseAuthentication no

# Change to no to disable tunnelled clear text passwords
#PasswordAuthentication yes

# Kerberos options
#KerberosAuthentication no
#KerberosGetAFSToken no
#KerberosOrLocalPasswd yes
#KerberosTicketCleanup yes

# GSSAPI options
#GSSAPIAuthentication no
#GSSAPICleanupCredentials yes
```

X11Forwarding yes
X11DisplayOffset 10
PrintMotd no
PrintLastLog yes
TCPKeepAlive yes
#UseLogin no

#MaxStartups 10:30:60
#Banner /etc/issue.net

Allow client to pass locale environment variables
AcceptEnv LANG LC_*

Subsystem sftp /usr/lib/openssh/sftp-server

Set this to 'yes' to enable PAM authentication, account processing,
and session processing. If this is enabled, PAM authentication will
be allowed through the ChallengeResponseAuthentication and
PasswordAuthentication. Depending on your PAM configuration,
PAM authentication via ChallengeResponseAuthentication may bypass
the setting of "PermitRootLogin without-password".
If you just want the PAM account and session checks to run without
PAM authentication, then enable this but set PasswordAuthentication
and ChallengeResponseAuthentication to 'no'.
UsePAM yes

/* ---------------------------
    /etc/vsftpd.chroot_list
---------------------------- */
xcanpcrunchx

/* ---------------------------
    /etc/vsftpd.chroot_list
---------------------------- */
    Nota: Dejar este archivo en blanco.

/* ---------------------
    /etc/vsftpd.conf
---------------------- */
#Example config file /etc/vsftpd.conf
#
The default compiled in settings are fairly paranoid. This sample file
loosens things up a bit, to make the ftp daemon more usable.

```
# Please see vsftpd.conf.5 for all compiled in defaults.
#
# READ THIS: This example file is NOT an exhaustive list of vsftpd
options.
# Please read the vsftpd.conf.5 manual page to get a full idea of vsftpd's
# capabilities.
#
#
# Run standalone? vsftpd can run either from an inetd or as a standalone
# daemon started from an initscript.
#listen=YES
listen=NO
#
# Run standalone with IPv6?
# Like the listen parameter, except vsftpd will listen on an IPv6 socket
# instead of an IPv4 one. This parameter and the listen parameter are
mutually
# exclusive.
#listen_ipv6=YES
#
# Allow anonymous FTP? (Beware - allowed by default if you comment
this out).
# <<< NEXT OPTION UPDATED! >>>
#anonymous_enable=YES
#
# Uncomment this to allow local users to log in.
# <<< NEXT OPTION UPDATED! >>>
local_enable=YES
#
# Uncomment this to enable any form of FTP write command.
write_enable=YES
#
# Default umask for local users is 077. You may wish to change this to 022,
# if your users expect that (022 is used by most other ftpd's)
# <<< NEXT OPTION UPDATED! >>>
local_umask=022
#
# Uncomment this to allow the anonymous FTP user to upload files. This
only
# has an effect if the above global write enable is activated. Also, you will
# obviously need to create a directory writable by the FTP user.
anon_upload_enable=YES
#
```

# Uncomment this if you want the anonymous FTP user to be able to create
# new directories.
anon_mkdir_write_enable=YES
#
Activate directory messages - messages given to remote users when they
go into a certain directory.
<<< NEXT OPTION UPDATED >>>
#dirmessage_enable=YES
#
# Activate logging of uploads/downloads.
xferlog_enable=YES
#
# Make sure PORT transfer connections originate from port 20 (ftp-data).
connect_from_port_20=YES
#
If you want, you can arrange for uploaded anonymous files to be owned by
a different user. Note! Using "root" for uploaded files is not
recommended!
#chown_uploads=YES
#chown_username=whoever
#
You may override where the log file goes if you like. The default is shown
below.
#xferlog_file=/var/log/vsftpd.log
#
If you want, you can have your log file in standard ftpd xferlog format
#xferlog_std_format=YES
#
# You may change the default value for timing out an idle session.
# <<< NEXT OPTION UPDATED! >>>
idle_session_timeout=600
#
# You may change the default value for timing out a data connection.
# <<< NEXT OPTION UPDATED! >>>
data_connection_timeout=300
#
It is recommended that you define on your system a unique user which the
ftp server can use as a totally isolated and unprivileged user.
#nopriv_user=ftpsecure
#

# Enable this and the server will recognise asynchronous ABOR requests. Not
# recommended for security (the code is non-trivial). Not enabling it,
# however, may confuse older FTP clients.
# <<< NEXT LINE UPDATED! >>>
async_abor_enable=YES
#
By default the server will pretend to allow ASCII mode but in fact ignore
the request. Turn on the below options to have the server actually do ASCII
mangling on files when in ASCII mode.
Beware that on some FTP servers, ASCII support allows a denial of service
attack (DoS) via the command "SIZE /big/file" in ASCII mode. vsftpd
predicted this attack and has always been safe, reporting the size of the
raw file.
ASCII mangling is a horrible feature of the protocol.
#ascii_upload_enable=YES
#ascii_download_enable=YES
#
# You may fully customise the login banner string:
# <<< NEXT LINE UPDATED! >>>
ftpd_banner=Welcome to aestudio.sytes.net FTP service.
#
You may specify a file of disallowed anonymous e-mail addresses. Apparently
useful for combatting certain DoS attacks.
#deny_email_enable=YES
(default follows)
#banned_email_file=/etc/vsftpd.banned_emails
#
# You may restrict local users to their home directories. See the FAQ for
# the possible risks in this before using chroot_local_user or
# chroot_list_enable below.
chroot_local_user=YES
#chroot_loca_users=YES
#chrott_local_users=YES

#
You may specify an explicit list of local users to chroot() to their home
directory. If chroot_local_user is YES, then this list becomes a list of
users to NOT chroot().
<<< NEXT LINE UPDATED! >>>

```
chroot_list_enable=YES
# (default follows)
# <<< NEXT LINE UPDATED >>>
chroot_list_file=/etc/vsftpd.chroot_list
#
# You may activate the "-R" option to the builtin ls. This is disabled by
# default to avoid remote users being able to cause excessive I/O on large
# sites. However, some broken FTP clients such as "ncftp" and "mirror"
assume
# the presence of the "-R" option, so there is a strong case for enabling it.
#ls_recurse_enable=YES
#
#
# Debian customization
#
# Some of vsftpd's settings don't fit the Debian filesystem layout by
# default.  These settings are more Debian-friendly.
#
# This option should be the name of a directory which is empty.  Also, the
# directory should not be writable by the ftp user. This directory is used
# as a secure chroot() jail at times vsftpd does not require filesystem
# access.
secure_chroot_dir=/var/run/vsftpd
#
# This string is the name of the PAM service vsftpd will use.
pam_service_name=vsftpd
#
# This option specifies the location of the RSA certificate to use for SSL
# encrypted connections.
rsa_cert_file=/etc/ssl/certs/vsftpd.pem

# --== New added lines ==--
force_dot_files=NO
guest_enable=NO
hide_ids=YES
pasv_min_port=50000
pasv_max_port=60000
one_process_model=NO
accept_timeout=60
connect_timeout=300
max_per_ip=4
userlist_enable=YES
tcp_wrappers=YES
```

```
# The maximum data transfer rate permitted, in bytes per second,
# for local authenticated users:
#local_max_rate=10000

/* ---------------------------------
        /var/lib/libvirt/qemu/x2.xml
------------------------------------ */
<domain type='kvm'>
 <name>x2</name>
 <uuid>fcb926c0-cd64-4af9-9718-5b5712067388</uuid>
 <memory>390000</memory>
 <currentMemory>390000</currentMemory>
 <vcpu>2</vcpu>
 <os>
  <type arch='i686' machine='pc'>hvm</type>
  <boot dev='hd'/>
 </os>
 <features>
  <acpi/>
 </features>
 <clock offset='utc'/>
 <on_poweroff>destroy</on_poweroff>
 <on_reboot>restart</on_reboot>
 <on_crash>destroy</on_crash>
 <devices>
  <emulator>/usr/bin/kvm</emulator>
  <disk type='file' device='cdrom'>
    <driver name='qemu' type='raw'/>
    <source file='/var/lib/libvirt/images/KNOPPIX_V7.0.5DVD-2012-
12-21-EN.iso'/>
    <target dev='hdc' bus='ide'/>
    <readonly/>
    <address type='drive' controller='0' bus='1' unit='0'/>
  </disk>
  <disk type='file' device='disk'>
<driver name='qemu' type='qcow2'/>
    <source file='/var/lib/libvirt/images/x2.qcow2'/>
    <target dev='hda' bus='scsi'/>
  </disk>
 <interface type='bridge'>
    <mac address='00:50:56:3E:06:0B'/>
    <source bridge='br0'/>
    </interface>
```

```
<interface type='bridge'>
    <mac address='00:50:56:2A:04:3A'/>
    <source bridge='br0'/>
    </interface>
<interface type='bridge'>
    <mac address='00:50:56:3D:F8:0E'/>
    <source bridge='br0'/>
    </interface>
<interface type='bridge'>
    <mac address='00:50:56:36:4F:EC'/>
    <source bridge='br0'/>
    </interface>
<interface type='bridge'>
    <mac address='00:50:56:32:52:C1'/>
    <source bridge='br0'/>
    </interface>
  <input type='mouse' bus='ps2'/>
  <graphics type='vnc' port='-1' listen='127.0.0.1'/>
 </devices>
</domain>


/* -----------------------
     /etc/apt/sources.list
--------------------------- */
#

# deb cdrom:[Debian GNU/Linux 6.0.6 _Squeeze_ - Official Multi-
architecture amd64/i386 NETINST #1 20120930-16:04]/ squeeze main

#deb cdrom:[Debian GNU/Linux 6.0.6 _Squeeze_ - Official Multi-
architecture amd64/i386 NETINST #1 20120930-16:04]/ squeeze main

deb http://ftp.us.debian.org/debian/ squeeze main
deb-src http://ftp.us.debian.org/debian/ squeeze main

#deb http://security.debian.org/ squeeze/updates main
#deb-src http://security.debian.org/ squeeze/updates main

# squeeze-updates, previously known as 'volatile'
deb http://ftp.us.debian.org/debian/ squeeze-updates main
deb-src http://ftp.us.debian.org/debian/ squeeze-updates main

# Line to add unrar non-free
```

#deb http://ftp.de.debian.org/debian sid main non-free

En el espacio de root:
N/A

En el espacio de usuario:
N/A

No se ha agregado ningún archivo de configurado para las versiones previas de foobar con servidores de virtualización VMware® Workstation ni Virtual Box® en este libro, debido a que las interfaces gráficas de sus respectivos programas generan dichos archivos y se ha optado por la migración hacia la virtualización KVM, nativa de Linux, al final del proyecto.
No se han agregado los archivos que se crean mediante comandos para conectar hosts foobar como servidor virtual de Virtual Machine Manager para KVM con ssh en el host vgui, que son id_dsa.pub y id_dsa del directorio /root y authorized_keys del directorio /root/.ssh/, y id_dsa.pub del directorio .ssh/ del usuario xcapncrunchx (Ver DVD LE SF 3 para configurar el cliente de Virtualización KVM en el host vgui).
No se han agregado los archivos de configurado de programas de seguridad para foobar que también serán necesarios dependiendo del tipo de configuración del ambiente. En caso de usar un servidor bastión, entre más aislado y seguro mejor. La mayoría de estos archivos son similares a los de los host aestudio o x2, por ejemplo: Script de firewall de iptables, que debe tomar en cuenta servicios como FTP y cerrar casi todos los puertos por default (Esto se aprende en el DVD LE SF 1 en el videoprograma de firewall y se retoma en distintas secciones del proyecto), o los archivos de configurado de Tripwire. Fail2ban es necesario para asegurar en cierta medida ssh y se debe configurar para evitar ciertos ataques DOS y DDOS desde Internet si es que queremos tener proxy, KVM server y en general se recomienda para todo servidor foobar accesible desde Internet. En caso de tener foobar u otro servidor de la clase foobar como proxy se debe prescindir del firewall o modificarlo para redireccionar todos los paquetes a servicios como el http en el puerto 80 de los servidores del cluster configurados en máxima disponibilidad para por ejemplo crear una nube de servicios o servicios web (todo esto se explica en los DVD de LE SF).

Host: x2.
Función: Servidor en granja de servidores o cluster HA de máxima disponibilidad basado en el servidor bastión stand-alone aestudio con todos los servicios disponibles.
Archivos modificados o creados:

En el sistema:
```
/* ----------------------------------------
        /var/www/passwd/.aestudio.sytes.net
----------------------------------------- */
```
Nota: En este archivo el comando passwd crea una entrada con el nombre de usuario, luego dos puntos y luego una clave encriptada que lee el Apache Web Server cuando el usuario para buscar los usuario con acceso htaccess. Ver el archivo .htaccess en este libro.
aestudio:dfdfjUrer84RF


```
/* -----------------------------------------------------
        /home/aestudio/public_html/private_dir/.htaccess
----------------------------------------------------- */
AuthType basic
AuthUserFile /var/www/passwd/.aestudio.sytes.net
AuthName "Restricted"
<LIMIT GET POST>
require valid-user
</LIMIT>
```

```
/* ----------------------------
        /etc/boot/grub/menu.lst
---------------------------- */
```
Nota: Este es el archivo de configurado de la versión Debian GNU/Linux de grub1, Grub Legacy. Para la versión Squeeze de Debian existe la posibilidad de elegir entre Legacy o Grub2. A partir de la versión de Debian Wheezy sólo se permite instalar Grub2. Algunas veces el futuro del "open source" es incierto, lo mismo que el de su configuración. Ver el archivo de configurado de Grub2 en este libro (Se ejemplifica con el host foobar).
```
# menu.lst - See: grub(8), info grub, update-grub(8)
#         grub-install(8), grub-floppy(8),
#         grub-md5-crypt, /usr/share/doc/grub
#         and /usr/share/doc/grub-doc/.

## default num
# Set the default entry to the entry number NUM. Numbering starts from 0, and
# the entry number 0 is the default if the command is not used.
#
# You can specify 'saved' instead of a number. In this case, the default entry
# is the entry saved with the command 'savedefault'.
```

WARNING: If you are using dmraid do not change this entry to 'saved' or your
array will desync and will not let you boot your system.
default   0

timeout sec
Set a timeout, in SEC seconds, before automatically booting the default entry
(normally the first entry defined).
timeout   5

Pretty colours
color cyan/blue white/blue

password ['--md5'] passwd
If used in the first section of a menu file, disable all interactive editing
control (menu entry editor and command-line) and entries protected by the
command 'lock'
e.g. password SECRET-PASS_STRING
password --md5 1gLhU0/$aW78kHK1QfV3P2b2znUoe/
 password ROOT-PASS_HERE

#
examples
#
title   Windows 95/98/NT/2000
root   (hd0,0)
makeactive
chainloader +1
#
title   Linux
root   (hd0,1)
kernel   /vmlinuz root=/dev/hda2 ro
#

#
Put static boot stanzas before and/or after AUTOMAGIC KERNEL LIST

BEGIN AUTOMAGIC KERNELS LIST
lines between the AUTOMAGIC KERNELS LIST markers will be modified

by the debian update-grub script except for the default options below

DO NOT UNCOMMENT THEM, Just edit them to your needs

Start Default Options
default kernel options
default kernel options for automagic boot options
If you want special options for specific kernels use kopt_x_y_z
where x.y.z is kernel version. Minor versions can be omitted.
e.g. kopt=root=/dev/hda1 ro
kopt_2_6_8=root=/dev/hdc1 ro
kopt_2_6_8_2_686=root=/dev/hdc2 ro
kopt=root=/dev/sda1 ro

default grub root device
e.g. groot=(hd0,0)
groot=(hd0,0)

should update-grub create alternative automagic boot options
e.g. alternative=true
alternative=false
alternative=true

should update-grub lock alternative automagic boot options
e.g. lockalternative=true
lockalternative=false
lockalternative=false

additional options to use with the default boot option, but not with the
alternatives
e.g. defoptions=vga=791 resume=/dev/hda5
defoptions=

should update-grub lock old automagic boot options
e.g. lockold=false
lockold=true
lockold=false

Xen hypervisor options to use with the default Xen boot option
xenhopt=

Xen Linux kernel options to use with the default Xen boot option
xenkopt=console=tty0

```
## altoption boot targets option
## multiple altoptions lines are allowed
## e.g. altoptions=(extra menu suffix) extra boot options
##     altoptions=(single-user) single
# altoptions=(single-user mode) single


## controls how many kernels should be put into the menu.lst
## only counts the first occurence of a kernel, not the
## alternative kernel options
## e.g. howmany=all
##     howmany=7
# howmany=all


## should update-grub create memtest86 boot option
## e.g. memtest86=true
##     memtest86=false
# memtest86=true


## should update-grub adjust the value of the default booted system
## can be true or false
# updatedefaultentry=false


## should update-grub add savedefault to the default options
## can be true or false
# savedefault=false


## ## End Default Options ##


title       Debian GNU/Linux, kernel 2.6.26-2-686
root        (hd0,0)
kernel          /boot/vmlinuz-2.6.26-2-686 root=/dev/sda1 ro
initrd          /boot/initrd.img-2.6.26-2-686

title       Debian GNU/Linux, kernel 2.6.26-2-686 (single-user mode)
root        (hd0,0)
kernel          /boot/vmlinuz-2.6.26-2-686 root=/dev/sda1 ro single
initrd          /boot/initrd.img-2.6.26-2-686

title       Debian GNU/Linux, kernel 2.6.18-4-686
root        (hd0,0)
kernel          /boot/vmlinuz-2.6.18-4-686 root=/dev/sda1 ro
initrd          /boot/initrd.img-2.6.18-4-686
```

```
title       Debian GNU/Linux, kernel 2.6.18-4-686 (single-user mode)
root        (hd0,0)
kernel          /boot/vmlinuz-2.6.18-4-686 root=/dev/sda1 ro single
initrd          /boot/initrd.img-2.6.18-4-686
```

END DEBIAN AUTOMAGIC KERNELS LIST

```
/* ----------------------------------------------
      /etc/amavis/conf.d/15-content_filter_mode
---------------------------------------------- */
use strict;
```

\# You can modify this file to re-enable SPAM checking through spamassassin
\# and to re-enable antivirus checking.

```
#
# Default antivirus checking mode
# Uncomment the two lines below to enable it back
#
```

```
@bypass_virus_checks_maps = (
  \%bypass_virus_checks,                    \@bypass_virus_checks_acl,
\$bypass_virus_checks_re);
```

```
#
# Default SPAM checking mode
# Uncomment the two lines below to enable it back
#
```

```
@bypass_spam_checks_maps = (
  \%bypass_spam_checks,                     \@bypass_spam_checks_acl,
\$bypass_spam_checks_re);
```

1; # ensure a defined return

```
/* -------------------------------
      /etc/amavis/conf.d/50-user
------------------------------- */
      Nota: Este es un ejemplo del archivo.
# The line "$sa_spam_subject_tag = undef;" is set to quit the
```

"***Spam***" brand of the mails.

The line "$sa_tag_level_deflt = undef;" is set because we want all the mails flagged with

the spam flags, so a mail will be sent to spam destiny while it has a big spam score in the

flags, for example, something like ************************.

The line "$final_spam_destiny = D_PASS;" is set to let mail pass to mailboxes. That way the

users will be able to look up the spam to find important mail in the spam folder, that is

probably marked as spam, because of the strong (but configurable, in the other line tag2)

spamming filters, including Bayesian filters. With the default 'D_BOUNCE' value, the users

can lost important mail, coming in the spam.

The "$spam_quarantine_to = undef;" is set because we are not defining a specific file to

send spamming, like the file is possible to be created in the filesystem.

#

Look the "editable" section and add your new changes.

#

--== New lines ==--

$sa_spam_subject_tag = undef;

$sa_tag_level_deflt = undef;

$final_spam_destiny = D_PASS;

$spam_quarantine_to = undef;

#

/* -------------------------------
        /etc/amavis/conf.d/50-user
------------------------------- */

Nota: Este es un segundo ejemplo del archivo, aunque podemos combinar todas las opciones de usuario dentro de un solo archivo (Ver videoprogramas de Servidor de Correo Electrónico en DVD LE SF 1).

Tell AmaVis "Do not consider as spamming the mail that is outgoing from one of our virtual

domains". Otherwise the mail will be considered spamming by the MTA servers and the destiny

servers, before it is scanned by server's destiny. Edit the file /etc/amavis/conf.d/50-user:

Add next lines at the end of the edition's part:

#

@lookup_sql_dsn = (

```
['DBI:mysql:database=mailserver;host=127.0.0.1;port=3306',
 'mailuser',
 'mailuser-pass-here']);
```

$sql_select_policy = 'SELECT name FROM virtual_domains WHERE CONCAT("@",name) IN (%k)';
#
#
Remember to set your own password, in the part of extract of the file where is the word
'mailuser-pass-here'.
The query will search the domain part from in the complete email address.

```
/* ---------------------------------------------------
     /etc/apache2/sites-enabled/aestudio.sytes.net
--------------------------------------------------- */
NameVirtualHost *:80

<VirtualHost *:80>
      ServerAdmin webmaster@localhost
      ServerName non.availa.ble
      ServerAlias non.availa.ble

      DocumentRoot /home/aestudio/null/
      <Directory />
           Options FollowSymLinks
           AllowOverride None
      </Directory>
      <Directory /home/aestudio/>
           Options Indexes FollowSymLinks MultiViews
           AllowOverride None
           Order allow,deny
           allow from all
           # RedirectMatch ^/$ /www/
      </Directory>

      ScriptAlias /cgi-bin/ /usr/lib/cgi-bin/
      <Directory "/usr/lib/cgi-bin">
           AllowOverride None
           Options +ExecCGI -MultiViews +SymLinksIfOwnerMatch
           Order allow,deny
           Allow from all
```

```
    </Directory>

    ErrorLog /var/log/apache2/error.log

    # Possible values include: debug, info, notice, warn, error, crit,
    # alert, emerg.
    LogLevel warn

    CustomLog /var/log/apache2/access.log combined

  Alias /doc/ "/usr/share/doc/"
  <Directory "/usr/share/doc/">
    Options Indexes MultiViews FollowSymLinks
    AllowOverride None
    Order deny,allow
    Deny from all
    Allow from 127.0.0.0/255.0.0.0 ::1/128
  </Directory>

</VirtualHost>


<VirtualHost *:80>
    ServerAdmin webmaster@localhost
    ServerName aestudio.sytes.net
    ServerAlias aestudio.xxz

    DocumentRoot /home/aestudio/public_html/
    <Directory />
        Options FollowSymLinks
        AllowOverride None
    </Directory>
    <Directory /home/aestudio/>
        Options Indexes FollowSymLinks MultiViews
        AllowOverride None
        Order allow,deny
        allow from all
        # RedirectMatch ^/$ /www/
    </Directory>

    ScriptAlias /cgi-bin/ /usr/lib/cgi-bin/
    <Directory "/usr/lib/cgi-bin">
        AllowOverride None
```

```
        Options +ExecCGI -MultiViews +SymLinksIfOwnerMatch
        Order allow,deny
        Allow from all
    </Directory>

    ErrorLog /var/log/apache2/error.log

    # Possible values include: debug, info, notice, warn, error, crit,
    # alert, emerg.
    LogLevel warn

    CustomLog /var/log/apache2/aestudio.sytes.net.log combined

  Alias /doc/ "/usr/share/doc/"
  <Directory "/usr/share/doc/">
    Options Indexes MultiViews FollowSymLinks
    AllowOverride None
    Order deny,allow
    Deny from all
    Allow from 127.0.0.0/255.0.0.0 ::1/128
  </Directory>

</VirtualHost>

/* ------------------------------------------------------
     /etc/apache2/sites-enabled/aestudio.sytes.net-tls
   ------------------------------------------------------ */
NameVirtualHost *:443

<VirtualHost *:443>
    ServerAdmin webmaster@localhost
    ServerName non.availa.ble
    ServerAlias non.availa.ble

    SSLEngine On
    SSLCertificateFile /etc/apache2/apache.pem
    SSLCertificateKeyFile /etc/apache2/apache.pem
    # SSLCertificateFile /var/www/sharedip/ssl/192.168.1.6.crt
    # SSLCertificateKeyFile /var/www/sharedip/ssl/192.168.1.6.key
    DocumentRoot /home/aestudio/null/
    <Directory />
        Options FollowSymLinks
        AllowOverride None
```

```
    </Directory>
    <Directory /home/aestudio/>
        Options Indexes FollowSymLinks MultiViews
        AllowOverride None
        Order allow,deny
        allow from all
        #RedirectMatch ^/$ /www/
    </Directory>

    ScriptAlias /cgi-bin/ /usr/lib/cgi-bin/
    <Directory "/usr/lib/cgi-bin">
        AllowOverride None
        Options +ExecCGI -MultiViews +SymLinksIfOwnerMatch
        Order allow,deny
        Allow from all
    </Directory>

    ErrorLog /var/log/apache2/error.log

    # Possible values include: debug, info, notice, warn, error, crit,
    # alert, emerg.
    LogLevel warn

    CustomLog /var/log/apache2/aestudio.sytes.net.log combined

  Alias /doc/ "/usr/share/doc/"
  <Directory "/usr/share/doc/">
    Options Indexes MultiViews FollowSymLinks
    AllowOverride None
    Order deny,allow
    Deny from all
    Allow from 127.0.0.0/255.0.0.0 ::1/128
  </Directory>

</VirtualHost>


<VirtualHost *:443>
        ServerAdmin webmaster@localhost
        ServerName aestudio.sytes.net
        ServerAlias aestudio

        SSLEngine On
```

```
SSLCertificateFile /etc/apache2/apache.pem
SSLCertificateKeyFile /etc/apache2/apache.pem
# SSLCertificateFile /var/www/sharedip/ssl/192.168.1.6.crt
# SSLCertificateKeyFile /var/www/sharedip/ssl/192.168.1.6.key
DocumentRoot /home/aestudio/public_html/
<Directory />
    Options FollowSymLinks
    AllowOverride None
</Directory>
<Directory /home/aestudio/>
    Options Indexes FollowSymLinks MultiViews
    AllowOverride None
    Order allow,deny
    allow from all
    #RedirectMatch ^/$ /www/
</Directory>

ScriptAlias /cgi-bin/ /usr/lib/cgi-bin/
<Directory "/usr/lib/cgi-bin">
    AllowOverride None
    Options +ExecCGI -MultiViews +SymLinksIfOwnerMatch
    Order allow,deny
    Allow from all
</Directory>

ErrorLog /var/log/apache2/error.log

# Possible values include: debug, info, notice, warn, error, crit,
# alert, emerg.
LogLevel warn

CustomLog /var/log/apache2/aestudio.sytes.net.log combined

Alias /doc/ "/usr/share/doc/"
<Directory "/usr/share/doc/">
  Options Indexes MultiViews FollowSymLinks
  AllowOverride None
  Order deny,allow
  Deny from all
  Allow from 127.0.0.0/255.0.0.0 ::1/128
</Directory>

</VirtualHost>
```

```
/* --------------------------------------------------
      /etc/apache2/sites-enabled/etribe.sytes.net
-------------------------------------------------- */
NameVirtualHost *:80

<VirtualHost *:80>
      ServerAdmin webmaster@localhost
      ServerName non.availa.ble
      ServerAlias non.availa.ble

      DocumentRoot /home/aestudio/null/
      <Directory />
            Options FollowSymLinks
            AllowOverride None
      </Directory>
      <Directory /home/aestudio/>
            Options Indexes FollowSymLinks MultiViews
            AllowOverride None
            Order allow,deny
            allow from all
            # RedirectMatch ^/$ /www/
      </Directory>

      ScriptAlias /cgi-bin/ /usr/lib/cgi-bin/
      <Directory "/usr/lib/cgi-bin">
            AllowOverride None
            Options +ExecCGI -MultiViews +SymLinksIfOwnerMatch
            Order allow,deny
            Allow from all
      </Directory>

      ErrorLog /var/log/apache2/error.log

      # Possible values include: debug, info, notice, warn, error, crit,
      # alert, emerg.
      LogLevel warn

      CustomLog /var/log/apache2/access.log combined

   Alias /doc/ "/usr/share/doc/"
   <Directory "/usr/share/doc/">
      Options Indexes MultiViews FollowSymLinks
```

```
        AllowOverride None
        Order deny,allow
        Deny from all
        Allow from 127.0.0.0/255.0.0.0 ::1/128
    </Directory>

</VirtualHost>


<VirtualHost *:80>
        ServerAdmin webmaster@localhost
        ServerName etribe.sytes.net
        ServerAlias aestudio.xxz

        DocumentRoot /home/etribe/public_html/
        <Directory />
            Options FollowSymLinks
            AllowOverride None
        </Directory>
        <Directory /home/etribe/>
            Options Indexes FollowSymLinks MultiViews
            AllowOverride None
            Order allow,deny
            allow from all
            # RedirectMatch ^/$ /www/
        </Directory>

        ScriptAlias /cgi-bin/ /usr/lib/cgi-bin/
        <Directory "/usr/lib/cgi-bin">
            AllowOverride None
            Options +ExecCGI -MultiViews +SymLinksIfOwnerMatch
            Order allow,deny
            Allow from all
        </Directory>

        ErrorLog /var/log/apache2/error.log

        # Possible values include: debug, info, notice, warn, error, crit,
        # alert, emerg.
        LogLevel warn

        CustomLog /var/log/apache2/etribe.sytes.net.log combined
```

```
Alias /doc/ "/usr/share/doc/"
<Directory "/usr/share/doc/">
    Options Indexes MultiViews FollowSymLinks
    AllowOverride None
    Order deny,allow
    Deny from all
    Allow from 127.0.0.0/255.0.0.0 ::1/128
</Directory>

</VirtualHost>

/* -----------------------------
       /etc/apache2/apache2.conf
------------------------------ */
```

Nota: Estas son las líneas agragadas al final del archivo. No se han considerado modificaciones en otras secciones importantes, como la activación de páginas personalizadas con mensajes de error como el error 404.

```
# --== New Lines ==--
DirectoryIndex index.html index.cgi index.pl index.php index.xhtml
index.shtml
#Lines at the end of the code, they go immediately after the last line:

Alias /awstatscss "/usr/share/doc/awstats/examples/css/"

Alias /awstatsicons "/usr/share/awstats/icon/"

ScriptAlias /awstats/ "/usr/lib/cgi-bin/"

Alias /awstats-icon/ /usr/share/awstats/icon/

<Directory /usr/share/awstats/icon>

Options None

AllowOverride None

Order allow,deny

Allow from all

</Directory>
```

#End of lines

```
/* ---------------------------
      /etc/apache2/httpd.conf
----------------------------- */
```

Nota: En este archivo, que al igual que todos los demás que editamos debe poseer un backup previo a su edición, pero además otro con la configuración predeterminada, es la versión final que se utilizará para habilitar o deshabilitar reglas de seguridad del módulo mod security de Apache2.

```
# Basic configuration options
SecRuleEngine On
SecRequestBodyAccess On
SecResponseBodyAccess Off

# Handling of file uploads
# TODO Choose a folder private to Apache.
# SecUploadDir /opt/apache-frontend/tmp/
SecUploadKeepFiles Off

# Debug log
SecDebugLog /var/log/a2-modsec-debug.log
SecDebugLogLevel 0

# Serial audit log
SecAuditEngine RelevantOnly
SecAuditLogRelevantStatus ^5
SecAuditLogParts ABIFHZ
SecAuditLogType Serial
SecAuditLog /var/log/a2-modsec-audit.log

# Maximum request body size we will
# accept for buffering
#SecRequestBodyLimit 131072
#--== Esteban line ==--
SecRequestBodyLimit 15728640


# Store up to 128 KB in memory
SecRequestBodyInMemoryLimit 131072

# Buffer response bodies of up to
# 512 KB in length
```

```
SecResponseBodyLimit 524288

# Verify that we've correctly processed the request body.
# As a rule of thumb, when failing to process a request body
# you should reject the request (when deployed in blocking mode)
# or log a high-severity alert (when deployed in detection-only mode).
SecRule REQBODY_PROCESSOR_ERROR "!@eq 0" \
"phase:2,t:none,log,deny,msg:'Failed to parse request body.',severity:2"

# By default be strict with what we accept in the multipart/form-data
# request body. If the rule below proves to be too strict for your
# environment consider changing it to detection-only. You are encouraged
# _not_ to remove it altogether.
SecRule MULTIPART_STRICT_ERROR "!@eq 0" \
"phase:2,t:none,log,deny,msg:'Multipart request body \
failed strict validation: \
PE %{REQBODY_PROCESSOR_ERROR}, \
BQ %{MULTIPART_BOUNDARY_QUOTED}, \
BW %{MULTIPART_BOUNDARY_WHITESPACE}, \
DB %{MULTIPART_DATA_BEFORE}, \
DA %{MULTIPART_DATA_AFTER}, \
HF %{MULTIPART_HEADER_FOLDING}, \
LF %{MULTIPART_LF_LINE}, \
SM %{MULTIPART_SEMICOLON_MISSING}'"

# Did we see anything that might be a boundary?
SecRule MULTIPART_UNMATCHED_BOUNDARY "!@eq 0" \
"phase:2,t:none,log,deny,msg:'Multipart    parser    detected    a    possible
unmatched boundary.'"

# --== New lines ==--
<IfModule mod_security2.c>
    #Include /etc/apache2/modsecurity_35_bad_robots.data
    #Include /etc/apache2/modsecurity_35_scanners.data
    #Include /etc/apache2/modsecurity_40_generic_attacks.data
    #Include /etc/apache2/modsecurity_41_sql_injection_attacks.data
    #Include /etc/apache2/modsecurity_42_comment_spam.data
    #Include /etc/apache2/modsecurity_46_et_sql_injection.data
    #Include /etc/apache2/modsecurity_46_et_web_rules.data
    #Include /etc/apache2/modsecurity_50_outbound.data
    #Include /etc/apache2/modsecurity_50_outbound_malware.data
    Include /etc/apache2/modsecurity_crs_10_config.conf
    Include /etc/apache2/modsecurity_crs_20_protocol_violations.conf
```

```
    Include /etc/apache2/modsecurity_crs_21_protocol_anomalies.conf
    Include /etc/apache2/modsecurity_crs_23_request_limits.conf
    Include /etc/apache2/modsecurity_crs_30_http_policy.conf
    Include /etc/apache2/modsecurity_crs_35_bad_robots.conf
    Include /etc/apache2/modsecurity_crs_40_experimental.conf
    Include /etc/apache2/modsecurity_crs_40_generic_attacks.conf
    Include /etc/apache2/modsecurity_crs_41_phpids_converter.conf
    Include /etc/apache2/modsecurity_crs_41_phpids_filters.conf
    Include /etc/apache2/modsecurity_crs_41_sql_injection_attacks.conf
    Include /etc/apache2/modsecurity_crs_41_xss_attacks.conf
    #Include /etc/apache2/modsecurity_crs_42_comment_spam.conf
    Include /etc/apache2/modsecurity_crs_42_tight_security.conf
    Include /etc/apache2/modsecurity_crs_45_trojans.conf
    Include /etc/apache2/modsecurity_crs_46_et_sql_injection.conf
    Include /etc/apache2/modsecurity_crs_46_et_web_rules.conf
    Include /etc/apache2/modsecurity_crs_47_common_exceptions.conf
    Include /etc/apache2/modsecurity_crs_48_local_exceptions.conf
    Include /etc/apache2/modsecurity_crs_49_enforcement.conf
    #Include /etc/apache2/modsecurity_crs_49_header_tagging.conf
    Include /etc/apache2/modsecurity_crs_49_inbound_blocking.conf
    Include /etc/apache2/modsecurity_crs_50_outbound.conf
    Include /etc/apache2/modsecurity_crs_55_marketing.conf
    Include /etc/apache2/modsecurity_crs_59_outbound_blocking.conf
    Include /etc/apache2/modsecurity_crs_60_correlation.conf
</IfModule>

/* ---------------------------
    /etc/apache2/ports.conf
------------------------------ */
# If you just change the port or add more ports here, you will likely also
# have to change the VirtualHost statement in
# /etc/apache2/sites-enabled/000-default
# This is also true if you have upgraded from before 2.2.9-3 (i.e. from
#        Debian        etch).        See        /usr/share/doc/apache2.2-
common/NEWS.Debian.gz and
# README.Debian.gz

NameVirtualHost *:80
Listen 80

<IfModule mod_ssl.c>
    # SSL name based virtual hosts are not yet supported, therefore no
    # NameVirtualHost statement here
```

Listen 443
</IfModule>

```
/* --------------------------
      /etc/apt/sources.list
-------------------------- */
#
# deb cdrom:[Debian GNU/Linux 4.0 r0 _Etch_ - Official i386 CD
Binary-1 20070407-11:55]/ etch contrib main

#deb cdrom:[Debian GNU/Linux 4.0 r0 _Etch_ - Official i386 CD Binary-
1 20070407-11:55]/ etch contrib main

# Line commented out by installer because it failed to verify:
#deb http://security.debian.org/ etch/updates main contrib
# Line commented out by installer because it failed to verify:
#deb-src http://security.debian.org/ etch/updates main contrib
#deb http://http.us.debian.org/debian etch main contrib non-free
#deb http://ftp.us.debian.org/debian/ lenny main contrib non-free
#deb-src http://ftp.us.debian.org/debian/ lenny main contrib non-free
#deb http://security.debian.org/ lenny/updates main contrib non-free

# Knoppix stable repo to be able to update Debian Lenny
#deb http://ftp.de.debian.org/pub/debian stable main contrib non-free

# Squeeze:
deb http://ftp.de.debian.org/debian/ squeeze main contrib non-free
deb-src http://ftp.de.debian.org/debian/ squeeze main contrib non-free

deb http://security.debian.org/ squeeze/updates main contrib non-free
deb-src http://security.debian.org/ squeeze/updates main contrib non-free

# squeeze-updates, previously known as 'volatile'
deb http://ftp.de.debian.org/debian/ squeeze-updates main contrib non-
free
deb-src http://ftp.de.debian.org/debian/ squeeze-updates main contrib
non-free

# Disabled because the line was affecting the apt-get update
#deb http://etc.inittab.org/~agi/debian/libapache-mod-security2/ ./

/* ------------------------------
      /etc/awstats/awstats.conf
```

------------------------------ */

Nota: Este archivo no se muestra completamente debido a su extensión. Además es un archivo predeterminado que luego funciona en el poyecto como base para crear los archivos de sitios. Ver archivo awstats.aestudio.sytes.net).

AWSTATS CONFIGURE FILE 6.95
#--
Copy this file into awstats.www.mydomain.conf and edit this new config file
to setup AWStats (See documentation in docs/ directory).
The config file must be in /etc/awstats, /usr/local/etc/awstats or /etc (for
Unix/Linux) or same directory than awstats.pl (Windows, Mac, Unix/Linux...)
To include an environment variable in any parameter (AWStats will replace
it with its value when reading it), follow the example:
Parameter="__ENVNAME__"
Note that environment variable AWSTATS_CURRENT_CONFIG is always defined with
the config value in an AWStats running session and can be used like others.
#--
$Revision: 1.338 $ - $Author: eldy $ - $Date: 2009/09/08 17:10:30 $

/* ------------------------------------
      /etc/awstats.aestudio.sytes.net
-------------------------------------- */

Nota: Este archivo no se muestra completamente debido a su extensión, pero se cubren todos los cambios realizados en él.

AWSTATS CONFIGURE FILE 6.6
#--
Copy this file into awstats.www.mydomain.conf and edit this new config file
to setup AWStats (See documentation in docs/ directory).
The config file must be in /etc/awstats, /usr/local/etc/awstats or /etc (for
Unix/Linux) or same directory than awstats.pl (Windows, Mac, Unix/Linux...)
To include an environment variable in any parameter (AWStats will replace
it with its value when reading it), follow the example:
Parameter="__ENVNAME__"

Note that environment variable AWSTATS_CURRENT_CONFIG is always defined with
the config value in an AWStats running session and can be used like others.
#--
$Revision: 1.327 $ - $Author: eldy $ - $Date: 2006/04/21 22:28:49 $

#--
MAIN SETUP SECTION (Required to make AWStats work)
#--
"LogFile" contains the web, ftp or mail server log file to analyze.
Possible values: A full path, or a relative path from awstats.pl directory.
Example: "/var/log/apache/access.log"
Example: "../logs/mycombinedlog.log"
You can also use tags in this filename if you need a dynamic file name
depending on date or time (Replacement is made by AWStats at the beginning
of its execution). This is available tags :
%YYYY-n is replaced with 4 digits year we were n hours ago
%YY-n   is replaced with 2 digits year we were n hours ago
%MM-n   is replaced with 2 digits month we were n hours ago
%MO-n   is replaced with 3 letters month we were n hours ago
%DD-n   is replaced with day we were n hours ago
%HH-n   is replaced with hour we were n hours ago
%NS-n   is replaced with number of seconds at 00:00 since 1970
%WM-n   is replaced with the week number in month (1-5)
%Wm-n   is replaced with the week number in month (0-4)
%WY-n   is replaced with the week number in year (01-52)
%Wy-n   is replaced with the week number in year (00-51)
%DW-n   is replaced with the day number in week (1-7, 1=sunday)
use n=24 if you need (1-7, 1=monday)
%Dw-n   is replaced with the day number in week (0-6, 0=sunday)
use n=24 if you need (0-6, 0=monday)
Use 0 for n if you need current year, month, day, hour...
Example: "/var/log/access_log.%YYYY-0%MM-0%DD-0.log"
Example: "C:/WINNT/system32/LogFiles/W3SVC1/ex%YY-24%MM-24%DD-24.log"
You can also use a pipe if log file come from a pipe :
Example: "gzip -d </var/log/apache/access.log.gz |"
If there are several log files from load balancing servers :
Example: "/pathtotools/logresolvemerge.pl *.log |"

```
#
LogFile="/var/log/apache2/aestudio.sytes.net.log"
```

```
# Enter the log file type you want to analyze.
# Possible values:
#  W - For a web log file
#  S - For a streaming log file
#  M - For a mail log file
#  F - For a ftp log file
# Example: W
# Default: W
#
LogType=W
```

```
# Enter here your log format (Must match your web server config. See setup
# instructions in documentation to know how to configure your web server to
# have the required log format).
# Possible values: 1,2,3,4 or "your_own_personalized_log_format"
# 1 - Apache or Lotus Notes/Domino native combined log format (NCSA combined/XLF/ELF log format)
# 2 - IIS or ISA format (IIS W3C log format). See FAQ-COM115 For ISA.
# 3 - Webstar native log format.
# 4 - Apache or Squid native common log format (NCSA common/CLF log format)
#      With LogFormat=4, some features (browsers, os, keywords...) can't work.
# "your_own_personalized_log_format" = If your log is ftp, mail or other format,
#      you must use following keys to define the log format string (See FAQ for
#      ftp, mail or exotic web log format examples):
#  %host          Client hostname or IP address (or Sender host for mail log)
#  %host_r        Receiver hostname or IP address (for mail log)
#  %lognamequot   Authenticated login/user with format: "john"
#  %logname       Authenticated login/user with format: john
#  %time1         Date and time with format: [dd/mon/yyyy:hh:mm:ss +0000] or [dd/mon/yyyy:hh:mm:ss]
#  %time2         Date and time with format: yyyy-mm-dd hh:mm:ss
```

```
#   %time3        Date and time with format: Mon dd hh:mm:ss or Mon
dd hh:mm:ss yyyy
#    %time4               Date and time with unix timestamp format:
dddddddddd
#   %methodurl      Method and URL with format: "GET /index.html
HTTP/x.x"
#   %methodurlnoprot Method and URL with format: "GET /index.html"
#   %method        Method with format: GET
#   %url           URL only with format: /index.html
#   %query         Query string (used by URLWithQuery option)
#   %code          Return code status (with format for web log: 999)
#   %bytesd        Size of document in bytes
#            %refererquot              Referer    page    with    format:
"http://from.com/from.htm"
#   %referer       Referer page with format: http://from.com/from.htm
#   %uabracket     User agent with format: [Mozilla/4.0 (compatible, ...)]
#   %uaquot        User agent with format: "Mozilla/4.0 (compatible, ...)"
#   %ua            User agent with format: Mozilla/4.0_(compatible...)
#   %gzipin        mod_gzip compression input bytes: In:XXX
#    %gzipout              mod_gzip compression output bytes & ratio:
Out:YYY:ZZpct.
#   %gzipratio     mod_gzip compression ratio: ZZpct.
#   %deflateratio  mod_deflate compression ratio with format: (ZZ)
#   %email         EMail sender (for mail log)
#   %email_r       EMail receiver (for mail log)
#   %virtualname   Web sever virtual hostname. Use this tag when same
log
#              contains data of several virtual web servers. AWStats
#              will discard records not in SiteDomain nor HostAliases
#   %cluster       If log file is provided from several computers (merged by
#              logresolvemerge.pl), use this to define cluster id field.
#   %extraX        Another field that you plan to use for building a
#              personalized report with ExtraSection feature (See later).
#   If your log format has some fields not included in this list, use:
#   %other         Means another not used field
#   %otherquot     Means another not used double quoted field
#
# Examples for Apache combined logs (following two examples are
equivalent):
# LogFormat = 1
# LogFormat = "%host %other %logname %time1 %methodurl %code
%bytesd %refererquot %uaquot"
#
```

```
# Example for IIS:
# LogFormat = 2
#
LogFormat=1
```

```
# If your log field's separator is not a space, you can change this parameter.
# This parameter is not used if LogFormat is a predefined value (1,2,3,4)
# Backslash can be used as escape character.
# Example: " "
# Example: "\t"
# Example: "\|"
# Example: ","
# Default: " "
#
LogSeparator=" "
```

```
# "SiteDomain" must contain the main domain name, or the main intranet
web
# server name, used to reach the web site.
# If you share the same log file for several virtual web servers, this
# parameter is used to tell AWStats to filter record that contains records for
# this virtual host name only (So check that this virtual hostname can be
# found in your log file and use a personalized log format that include the
# %virtualname tag).
# But for multi hosting a better solution is to have one log file for each
# virtual web server. In this case, this parameter is only used to generate
# full URL's links when ShowLinksOnUrl option is set to 1.
# If analyzing mail log, enter here the domain name of mail server.
# Example: "myintranetserver"
# Example: "www.domain.com"
# Example: "ftp.domain.com"
# Example: "domain.com"
#
SiteDomain="aestudio.sytes.net"
```

```
# Enter here all other possible domain names, addresses or virtual host
# aliases someone can use to access your site. Try to keep only the
minimum
# number of possible names/addresses to have the best performances.
# You can repeat the "SiteDomain" value in this list.
```

This parameter is used to analyze referer field in log file and to help
AWStats to know if a referer URL is a local URL of same site or an URL of
another site.
Note: Use space between each value.
Note: You can use regular expression values writing value with REGEX[value].
Note: You can also use @/mypath/myfile if list of aliases are in a file.
Example: "www.myserver.com   localhost   127.0.0.1
REGEX[mydomain\.(net|org)$]"
#
HostAliases="localhost 127.0.0.1"

If you want to have hosts reported by name instead of ip address, AWStats
need to make reverse DNS lookups (if not already done in your log file).
With DNSLookup to 0, all hosts will be reported by their IP addresses and
not by the full hostname of visitors (except if names are already available
in log file).
If you want/need to set DNSLookup to 1, don't forget that this will reduce
dramatically AWStats update process speed. Do not use on large web sites.
Note: Reverse DNS lookup is done on IPv4 only (Enable ipv6 plugin for IPv6).
Note: Result of DNS Lookup can be used to build the Country report. However
it is highly recommanded to enable the plugin 'geoipfree' or 'geoip' to
have an accurate Country report with no need of DNS Lookup.
Possible values:
0 - No DNS Lookup
1 - DNS Lookup is fully enabled
2 - DNS Lookup is made only from static DNS cache file (if it exists)
Default: 2
#
DNSLookup=0

When AWStats updates its statistics, it stores results of its analysis in
files (AWStats database). All those files are written in the directory
defined by the "DirData" parameter. Set this value to the directory where

you want AWStats to save its database and working files into.
Warning: If you want to be able to use the "AllowToUpdateStatsFromBrowser"
feature (see later), you need "Write" permissions by web server user on this
directory (and "Modify" for Windows NTFS file systems).
Example: "/var/lib/awstats"
Example: "../data"
Example: "C:/awstats_data_dir"
Default: "."   (means same directory as awstats.pl)
#
DirData="/var/lib/awstats"

Relative or absolute web URL of your awstats cgi-bin directory.
This parameter is used only when AWStats is run from command line
with -output option (to generate links in HTML reported page).
Example: "/awstats"
Default: "/cgi-bin"   (means awstats.pl is in "/yourwwwroot/cgi-bin")
#
DirCgi="/cgi-bin"

Relative or absolute web URL of your awstats icon directory.
If you build static reports ("... -output > outputpath/output.html"), enter
path of icon directory relative to the output directory 'outputpath'.
Example: "/awstatsicons"
Example: "../icon"
Default: "/icon" (means you must copy icon directories in "/mywwwroot/icon")
#
DirIcons="/awstats-icon"

When this parameter is set to 1, AWStats adds a button on report page to
allow to "update" statistics from a web browser. Warning, when "update" is
made from a browser, AWStats is run as a CGI by the web server user defined
in your web server (user "nobody" by default with Apache, "IUSR_XXX" with
IIS), so the "DirData" directory and all already existing history files
awstatsMMYYYY[.xxx].txt must be writable by this user. Change

permissions if
necessary to "Read/Write" (and "Modify" for Windows NTFS file systems).
Warning: Update process can be long so you might experience "time out"
browser errors if you don't launch AWStats frequently enough.
When set to 0, update is only made when AWStats is run from the command
line interface (or a task scheduler).
Possible values: 0 or 1
Default: 0
#
AllowToUpdateStatsFromBrowser=0

AWStats saves and sorts its database on a month basis (except if using
databasebreak option from command line).
However, if you choose the -month=all from command line or
value '-Year-' from CGI combo form to have a report for all year, AWStats
needs to reload all data for full year (each month), and sort them,
requiring a large amount of time, memory and CPU. This might be a problem
for web hosting providers that offer AWStats for large sites, on shared
servers, to non CPU cautious customers.
For this reason, the 'full year' is only enabled on Command Line by default.
You can change this by setting this parameter to 0, 1, 2 or 3.
Possible values:
0 - Never allowed
1 - Allowed on CLI only, -Year- value in combo is not visible
2 - Allowed on CLI only, -Year- value in combo is visible but not allowed
3 - Possible on CLI and CGI
Default: 2
#
AllowFullYearView=2

```
/* ----------------------------
      /etc/clamav/clamd.conf
---------------------------- */
```

Nota: este archivo no debe tocarse porque se genera automaticamente como muchos otros. Dentro del archivo se encuentra las instrucciones para reconfigurar el paquete con el programa dpkg.

```
/* ------------------------
        /etc/default/ntpdate
-------------------------- */
```
The settings in this file are used by the program ntpdate-debian, but not
by the upstream program ntpdate.

# Set to "yes" to take the server list from /etc/ntp.conf, from package ntp,
# so you only have to keep it in one place.
NTPDATE_USE_NTP_CONF=yes

# List of NTP servers to use (Separate multiple servers with spaces.)
# Not used if NTPDATE_USE_NTP_CONF is yes.
NTPSERVERS="0.debian.pool.ntp.org   1.debian.pool.ntp.org
2.debian.pool.ntp.org 3.debian.pool.ntp.org"

# Additional options to pass to ntpdate
NTPOPTIONS=""

```
/* -----------------------------
        /etc/dovecot/dovecot.conf
------------------------------- */
```
Dovecot configuration file

If you're in a hurry, see http://wiki.dovecot.org/QuickConfiguration

"dovecot -n" command gives a clean output of the changed settings. Use it
instead of copy&pasting this file when posting to the Dovecot mailing list.

'#' character and everything after it is treated as comments. Extra spaces
and tabs are ignored. If you want to use either of these explicitly, put the
value inside quotes, eg.: key = "# char and trailing whitespace "

Default values are shown for each setting, it's not required to uncomment
any of the lines. Exception to this are paths, they're just examples with
the real defaults being based on configure options. The paths listed here
are for configure --prefix=/usr --sysconfdir=/etc --localstatedir=/var
--with-ssldir=/etc/ssl

Base directory where to store runtime data.
#base_dir = /var/run/dovecot/

```
# Protocols we want to be serving: imap imaps pop3 pop3s managesieve
# If you only want to use dovecot-auth, you can set this to "none".
#protocols = imap imaps
protocols = imap imaps pop3 pop3s managesieve

# IP or host address where to listen in for connections. It's not currently
# possible to specify multiple addresses. "*" listens in all IPv4 interfaces.
# "[::]" listens in all IPv6 interfaces, but may also listen in all IPv4
# interfaces depending on the operating system.

# If you want to specify ports for each service, you will need to configure
# these settings inside the protocol imap/pop3/managesieve { ... } section,
# so you can specify different ports for IMAP/POP3/MANAGESIEVE.
For example:
#   protocol imap {
#     listen = *:10143
#     ssl_listen = *:10943
#     ..
#   }
#   protocol pop3 {
#     listen = *:10100
#     ..
#   }
#   protocol managesieve {
#     listen = *:12000
#     ..
#   }
#listen = *

# Disable LOGIN command and all other plaintext authentications unless
# SSL/TLS is used (LOGINDISABLED capability). Note that if the remote IP
# matches the local IP (ie. you're connecting from the same computer), the
# connection is considered secure and plaintext authentication is allowed.
disable_plaintext_auth = no

# Should all IMAP and POP3 processes be killed when Dovecot master process
# shuts down. Setting this to "no" means that Dovecot can be upgraded without
# forcing existing client connections to close (although that could also be
# a problem if the upgrade is eg. because of a security fix). This however
```

means that after master process has died, the client processes can't write
to log files anymore.
#shutdown_clients = yes

##
Logging
##

Log file to use for error messages, instead of sending them to syslog.
/dev/stderr can be used to log into stderr.
#log_path =

Log file to use for informational and debug messages.
Default is the same as log_path.
#info_log_path =

Prefix for each line written to log file. % codes are in strftime(3)
format.
#log_timestamp = "%b %d %H:%M:%S "
log_timestamp = "%Y-%m-%d %H:%M:%S "

Syslog facility to use if you're logging to syslog. Usually if you don't
want to use "mail", you'll use local0..local7. Also other standard
facilities are supported.
#syslog_facility = mail

##
SSL settings
##

IP or host address where to listen in for SSL connections. Defaults
to above if not specified.
#ssl_listen =

Disable SSL/TLS support.
#ssl_disable = no

PEM encoded X.509 SSL/TLS certificate and private key. They're opened before
dropping root privileges, so keep the key file unreadable by anyone but
root.
#ssl_cert_file = /etc/ssl/certs/dovecot.pem
#ssl_key_file = /etc/ssl/private/dovecot.pem

```
# If key file is password protected, give the password here. Alternatively
# give it when starting dovecot with -p parameter.
#ssl_key_password =

# File containing trusted SSL certificate authorities. Set this only if you
# intend to use ssl_verify_client_cert=yes. The CAfile should contain the
# CA-certificate(s) followed by the matching CRL(s).
#ssl_ca_file =

# Request client to send a certificate. If you also want to require it, set
# ssl_require_client_cert=yes in auth section.
#ssl_verify_client_cert = no

# How often to regenerate the SSL parameters file. Generation is quite
CPU
# intensive operation. The value is in hours, 0 disables regeneration
# entirely.
#ssl_parameters_regenerate = 168

# SSL ciphers to use
#ssl_cipher_list = ALL:!LOW

# Show protocol level SSL errors.
#verbose_ssl = no

##
## Login processes
##

# <doc/wiki/LoginProcess.txt>

# Directory where authentication process places authentication UNIX
sockets
# which login needs to be able to connect to. The sockets are created when
# running as root, so you don't have to worry about permissions. Note that
# everything in this directory is deleted when Dovecot is started.
#login_dir = /var/run/dovecot/login

# chroot login process to the login_dir. Only reason not to do this is if you
# wish to run the whole Dovecot without roots. <doc/wiki/Rootless.txt>
#login_chroot = yes
```

User to use for the login process. Create a completely new user for this,
and don't use it anywhere else. The user must also belong to a group where
only it has access, it's used to control access for authentication process.
Note that this user is NOT used to access mails. <doc/wiki/UserIds.txt>
#login_user = dovecot

Set max. process size in megabytes. If you don't use
login_process_per_connection you might need to grow this.
#login_process_size = 64

Should each login be processed in it's own process (yes), or should one
login process be allowed to process multiple connections (no)? Yes is more
secure, espcially with SSL/TLS enabled. No is faster since there's no need
to create processes all the time.
#login_process_per_connection = yes

Number of login processes to keep for listening new connections.
#login_processes_count = 3

Maximum number of login processes to create. The listening process count
usually stays at login_processes_count, but when multiple users start logging
in at the same time more extra processes are created. To prevent fork-bombing
we check only once in a second if new processes should be created - if all
of them are used at the time, we double their amount until the limit set by
this setting is reached.
#login_max_processes_count = 128

Maximum number of connections allowed per each login process. This setting
is used only if login_process_per_connection=no. Once the limit is reached,
the process notifies master so that it can create a new login process.
You should make sure that the process has at least
16 + login_max_connections * 2 available file descriptors.
#login_max_connections = 256

Greeting message for clients.
#login_greeting = Dovecot ready.

Space-separated list of elements we want to log. The elements which have
a non-empty variable value are joined together to form a comma-separated
string.
#login_log_format_elements = user=<%u> method=%m rip=%r lip=%l %c

Login log format. %$ contains login_log_format_elements string, %s contains
the data we want to log.
#login_log_format = %$: %s

##
Mailbox locations and namespaces
##

Location for users' mailboxes. This is the same as the old default_mail_env
setting. The default is empty, which means that Dovecot tries to find the
mailboxes automatically. This won't work if the user doesn't have any mail
yet, so you should explicitly tell Dovecot the full location.
#
If you're using mbox, giving a path to the INBOX file (eg. /var/mail/%u)
isn't enough. You'll also need to tell Dovecot where the other mailboxes are
kept. This is called the "root mail directory", and it must be the first
path given in the mail_location setting.
#
There are a few special variables you can use, eg.:
#
%u - username
%n - user part in user@domain, same as %u if there's no domain
%d - domain part in user@domain, empty if there's no domain
%h - home directory
#
See /usr/share/doc/dovecot-common/wiki/Variables.txt for full list.

Some
examples:
#
mail_location = maildir:~/Maildir
mail_location = mbox:~/mail:INBOX=/var/mail/%u
mail_location   =
mbox:/var/mail/%d/%1n/%n:INDEX=/var/indexes/%d/%1n/%n
#
<doc/wiki/MailLocation.txt>
#
mail_location = maildir:/var/vmail/%d/%n/Maildir

If you need to set multiple mailbox locations or want to change default
namespace settings, you can do it by defining namespace sections.
NOTE: Namespaces currently work ONLY with IMAP! POP3 and LDA currently ignore
namespaces completely, they use only the mail_location setting.
#
You can have private, shared and public namespaces. The only difference
between them is how Dovecot announces them to client via NAMESPACE
extension. Shared namespaces are meant for user-owned mailboxes which are
shared to other users, while public namespaces are for more globally
accessible mailboxes.
#
REMEMBER: If you add any namespaces, the default namespace must be added
explicitly, ie. mail_location does nothing unless you have a namespace
without a location setting. Default namespace is simply done by having a
namespace with empty prefix.
#namespace private {
   # Hierarchy separator to use. You should use the same separator for all
   # namespaces or some clients get confused. '/' is usually a good one.
   # The default however depends on the underlying mail storage format.
   #separator =

   # Prefix required to access this namespace. This needs to be different for
   # all namespaces. For example "Public/".
   #prefix =

   # Physical location of the mailbox. This is in same format as
   # mail_location, which is also the default for it.

```
#location =
```

```
# There can be only one INBOX, and this setting defines which namespace
# has it.
#inbox = yes
```

```
# If namespace is hidden, it's not advertised to clients via NAMESPACE
# extension or shown in LIST replies. This is mostly useful when converting
# from another server with different namespaces which you want to depricate
# but still keep working. For example you can create hidden namespaces with
# prefixes "~/mail/", "~%u/mail/" and "mail/".
#hidden = yes
#}
```

```
# Group to enable temporarily for privileged operations. Currently this is
# used only with INBOX when either its initial creation or dotlocking fails.
# Typically this is set to "mail" to give access to /var/mail.
mail_privileged_group = mail
```

```
# Grant access to these supplementary groups for mail processes. Typically
# these are used to set up access to shared mailboxes. Note that it may be
# dangerous to set these if users can create symlinks (e.g. if "mail" group is
# set here, ln -s /var/mail ~/mail/var could allow a user to delete others'
# mailboxes, or ln -s /secret/shared/box ~/mail/mybox would allow
reading it).
#mail_access_groups =
```

```
# Allow full filesystem access to clients. There's no access checks other than
# what the operating system does for the active UID/GID. It works with both
# maildir and mboxes, allowing you to prefix mailboxes names with eg. /path/
# or ~user/.
#mail_full_filesystem_access = no
```

```
##
## Mail processes
##
```

Enable mail process debugging. This can help you figure out why Dovecot
isn't finding your mails.
#mail_debug = no

Log prefix for mail processes.
See /usr/share/doc/dovecot-common/wiki/Variables.txt for list of possible
variables you can use.
#mail_log_prefix = "%Us(%u): "

Max. number of lines a mail process is allowed to log per second before it's
throttled. 0 means unlimited. Typically there's no need to change this
unless you're using mail_log plugin, which may log a lot.
#mail_log_max_lines_per_sec = 10

Don't use mmap() at all. This is required if you store indexes to shared
filesystems (NFS or clustered filesystem).
#mmap_disable = no

Don't write() to mmaped files. This is required for some operating systems
which use separate caches for them, such as OpenBSD.
#mmap_no_write = no

Rely on O_EXCL to work when creating dotlock files. The default is to use
hard linking. O_EXCL makes the dotlocking faster, but it doesn't always
work with NFS.
#dotlock_use_excl = no

Don't use fsync() or fdatasync() calls. This makes the performance better
at the cost of potential data loss if the server (or the file server)
goes down.
#fsync_disable = no

Locking method for index files. Alternatives are fcntl, flock and dotlock.
Dotlocking uses some tricks which may create more disk I/O than other locking
methods. NFS users: flock doesn't work, remember to change mmap_disable.

#lock_method = fcntl

Drop all privileges before exec()ing the mail process. This is mostly
meant for debugging, otherwise you don't get core dumps. It could be a small
security risk if you use single UID for multiple users, as the users could
ptrace() each others processes then.
#mail_drop_priv_before_exec = no

Show more verbose process titles (in ps). Currently shows user name and
IP address. Useful for seeing who are actually using the IMAP processes
(eg. shared mailboxes or if same uid is used for multiple accounts).
#verbose_proctitle = no

Valid UID range for users, defaults to 500 and above. This is mostly
to make sure that users can't log in as daemons or other system users.
Note that denying root logins is hardcoded to dovecot binary and can't
be done even if first_valid_uid is set to 0.
#first_valid_uid = 500
#last_valid_uid = 0

Valid GID range for users, defaults to non-root/wheel. Users having
non-valid GID as primary group ID aren't allowed to log in. If user
belongs to supplementary groups with non-valid GIDs, those groups are
not set.
#first_valid_gid = 1
#last_valid_gid = 0

Maximum number of running mail processes. When this limit is reached,
new users aren't allowed to log in.
#max_mail_processes = 1024

Set max. process size in megabytes. Most of the memory goes to mmap()ing
files, so it shouldn't harm much even if this limit is set pretty high.
#mail_process_size = 256

Maximum allowed length for mail keyword name. It's only forced when trying
to create new keywords.
#mail_max_keyword_length = 50

':' separated list of directories under which chrooting is allowed for mail

processes (ie. /var/mail will allow chrooting to /var/mail/foo/bar too).
This setting doesn't affect login_chroot or auth chroot variables.
WARNING: Never add directories here which local users can modify, that
may lead to root exploit. Usually this should be done only if you don't
allow shell access for users. <doc/wiki/Chrooting.txt>
#valid_chroot_dirs =

Default chroot directory for mail processes. This can be overridden for
specific users in user database by giving /./ in user's home directory
(eg. /home/./user chroots into /home). Note that usually there is no real
need to do chrooting, Dovecot doesn't allow users to access files outside
their mail directory anyway. <doc/wiki/Chrooting.txt>
#mail_chroot =

##
Mailbox handling optimizations
##

Space-separated list of fields to initially save into cache file. Currently
these fields are allowed:
#
flags, date.sent, date.received, size.virtual, size.physical
mime.parts, imap.body, imap.bodystructure
#
Different IMAP clients work in different ways, so they benefit from
different cached fields. Some do not benefit from them at all. Caching more
than necessary generates useless disk I/O, so you don't want to do that
either.
#
Dovecot attempts to automatically figure out what client wants and it keeps
only that. However the first few times a mailbox is opened, Dovecot hasn't
yet figured out what client needs, so it may not perform optimally. If you
know what fields the majority of your clients need, it may be useful to set
these fields by hand. If client doesn't actually use them, Dovecot will
eventually drop them.
#
Usually you should just leave this field alone. The potential benefits are
typically unnoticeable.
#mail_cache_fields =

Space-separated list of fields that Dovecot should never save to cache
file.
Useful if you want to save disk space at the cost of more I/O when the
fields
needed.
#mail_never_cache_fields =

The minimum number of mails in a mailbox before updates are done to
cache
file. This allows optimizing Dovecot's behavior to do less disk writes at
the cost of more disk reads.
#mail_cache_min_mail_count = 0

When IDLE command is running, mailbox is checked once in a while to
see if
there are any new mails or other changes. This setting defines the
minimum
time in seconds to wait between those checks. Dovecot can also use
dnotify,
inotify and kqueue to find out immediately when changes occur.
#mailbox_idle_check_interval = 30

Save mails with CR+LF instead of plain LF. This makes sending those
mails
take less CPU, especially with sendfile() syscall with Linux and FreeBSD.
But it also creates a bit more disk I/O which may just make it slower.
Also note that if other software reads the mboxes/maildirs, they may
handle
the extra CRs wrong and cause problems.
#mail_save_crlf = no

##
Maildir-specific settings
##

By default LIST command returns all entries in maildir beginning with a
dot.
Enabling this option makes Dovecot return only entries which are
directories.
This is done by stat()ing each entry, so it causes more disk I/O.
(For systems setting struct dirent->d_type, this check is free and it's
done always regardless of this setting)

#maildir_stat_dirs = no

When copying a message, do it with hard links whenever possible. This makes
the performance much better, and it's unlikely to have any side effects.
#maildir_copy_with_hardlinks = no

When copying a message, try to preserve the base filename. Only if the
destination mailbox already contains the same name (ie. the mail is being
copied there twice), a new name is given. The destination filename check is
done only by looking at dovecot-uidlist file, so if something outside
Dovecot does similar filename preserving copies, you may run into problems.
NOTE: This setting requires maildir_copy_with_hardlinks = yes to work.
#maildir_copy_preserve_filename = no

##
mbox-specific settings
##

Which locking methods to use for locking mbox. There are four available:
dotlock: Create <mailbox>.lock file. This is the oldest and most NFS-safe
solution. If you want to use /var/mail/ like directory, the users
will need write access to that directory.
fcntl : Use this if possible. Works with NFS too if lockd is used.
flock : May not exist in all systems. Doesn't work with NFS.
lockf : May not exist in all systems. Doesn't work with NFS.
#
You can use multiple locking methods; if you do the order they're declared
in is important to avoid deadlocks if other MTAs/MUAs are using multiple
locking methods as well. Some operating systems don't allow using some of
them simultaneously.
#mbox_read_locks = fcntl
#mbox_write_locks = dotlock fcntl

Maximum time in seconds to wait for lock (all of them) before aborting.

```
#mbox_lock_timeout = 300


# If dotlock exists but the mailbox isn't modified in any way, override the
# lock file after this many seconds.
#mbox_dotlock_change_timeout = 120


# When mbox changes unexpectedly we have to fully read it to find out
what
# changed. If the mbox is large this can take a long time. Since the change
# is usually just a newly appended mail, it'd be faster to simply read the
# new mails. If this setting is enabled, Dovecot does this but still safely
# fallbacks to re-reading the whole mbox file whenever something in mbox
isn't
# how it's expected to be. The only real downside to this setting is that if
# some other MUA changes message flags, Dovecot doesn't notice it
immediately.
# Note that a full sync is done with SELECT, EXAMINE, EXPUNGE
and CHECK
# commands.
#mbox_dirty_syncs = yes


# Like mbox_dirty_syncs, but don't do full syncs even with SELECT,
EXAMINE,
# EXPUNGE or CHECK commands. If this is set, mbox_dirty_syncs is
ignored.
#mbox_very_dirty_syncs = no


# Delay writing mbox headers until doing a full write sync (EXPUNGE
and CHECK
# commands and when closing the mailbox). This is especially useful for
POP3
# where clients often delete all mails. The downside is that our changes
# aren't immediately visible to other MUAs.
#mbox_lazy_writes = yes


# If mbox size is smaller than this (in kilobytes), don't write index files.
# If an index file already exists it's still read, just not updated.
#mbox_min_index_size = 0


##
## dbox-specific settings
##
```

Maximum dbox file size in kilobytes until it's rotated.
#dbox_rotate_size = 2048

Minimum dbox file size in kilobytes before it's rotated
(overrides dbox_rotate_days)
#dbox_rotate_min_size = 16

Maximum dbox file age in days until it's rotated. Day always begins from
midnight, so 1 = today, 2 = yesterday, etc. 0 = check disabled.
#dbox_rotate_days = 0

##
IMAP specific settings
##

protocol imap {
  # Login executable location.
  #login_executable = /usr/lib/dovecot/imap-login

  # IMAP executable location. Changing this allows you to execute other
  # binaries before the imap process is executed.
  #
  # This would write rawlogs into ~/dovecot.rawlog/ directory:
  #   mail_executable = /usr/lib/dovecot/rawlog /usr/lib/dovecot/imap
  #
  # This would attach gdb into the imap process and write backtraces into
  # /tmp/gdbhelper.* files:
  #   mail_executable   =   /usr/libexec/dovecot/gdbhelper
/usr/libexec/dovecot/imap
  #
  #mail_executable = /usr/lib/dovecot/imap

  # Maximum IMAP command line length in bytes. Some clients generate
very long
  # command lines with huge mailboxes, so you may need to raise this if
you get
  # "Too long argument" or "IMAP command line too large" errors often.
  #imap_max_line_length = 65536

  # Support for dynamically loadable plugins. mail_plugins is a space
separated
  # list of plugins to load.
  #mail_plugins =

```
mail_plugins = quota imap_quota
#mail_plugin_dir = /usr/lib/dovecot/modules/imap
```

Send IMAP capabilities in greeting message. This makes it unnecessary for
clients to request it with CAPABILITY command, so it saves one round-trip.
Many clients however don't understand it and ask the CAPABILITY anyway.
#login_greeting_capability = no

Override the IMAP CAPABILITY response.
#imap_capability =

Workarounds for various client bugs:
delay-newmail:
Send EXISTS/RECENT new mail notifications only when replying to NOOP
and CHECK commands. Some clients ignore them otherwise, for example OSX
Mail (<v2.1). Outlook Express breaks more badly though, without this it
may show user "Message no longer in server" errors. Note that OE6 still
breaks even with this workaround if synchronization is set to
"Headers Only".
outlook-idle:
Outlook and Outlook Express never abort IDLE command, so if no mail
arrives in half a hour, Dovecot closes the connection. This is still
fine, except Outlook doesn't connect back so you don't see if new mail
arrives.
netscape-eoh:
Netscape 4.x breaks if message headers don't end with the empty "end of
headers" line. Normally all messages have this, but setting this
workaround makes sure that Netscape never breaks by adding the line if
it doesn't exist. This is done only for FETCH BODY[HEADER.FIELDS..]
commands. Note that RFC says this shouldn't be done.
tb-extra-mailbox-sep:

```
  #       With mbox storage a mailbox can contain either mails or
submailboxes,
  #    but not both. Thunderbird separates these two by forcing server to
  #    accept '/' suffix in mailbox names in subscriptions list.
  # The list is space-separated.
  #imap_client_workarounds = outlook-idle
}

##
## POP3 specific settings
##

protocol pop3 {
  # Login executable location.
  #login_executable = /usr/lib/dovecot/pop3-login

  # POP3 executable location. See IMAP's mail_executable above for
examples
  # how this could be changed.
  #mail_executable = /usr/lib/dovecot/pop3

  # Don't try to set mails non-recent or seen with POP3 sessions. This is
  # mostly intended to reduce disk I/O. With maildir it doesn't move files
  # from new/ to cur/, with mbox it doesn't write Status-header.
  #pop3_no_flag_updates = no

  # Support LAST command which exists in old POP3 specs, but has been
removed
  # from new ones. Some clients still wish to use this though. Enabling this
  # makes RSET command clear all \Seen flags from messages.
  #pop3_enable_last = no

  # If mail has X-UIDL header, use it as the mail's UIDL.
  #pop3_reuse_xuidl = no

  # Keep the mailbox locked for the entire POP3 session.
  #pop3_lock_session = no

  # POP3 UIDL (unique mail identifier) format to use. You can use
following
  # variables:
  #
  # %v - Mailbox's IMAP UIDVALIDITY
```

```
#  %u - Mail's IMAP UID
#  %m - MD5 sum of the mailbox headers in hex (mbox only)
#  %f - filename (maildir only)
#
# If you want UIDL compatibility with other POP3 servers, use:
#  UW's ipop3d      : %08Xv%08Xu
#  Courier version 0  : %f
#  Courier version 1  : %u
#  Courier version 2  : %v-%u
#  Cyrus (<= 2.1.3)   : %u
#  Cyrus (>= 2.1.4)   : %v.%u
#  Older Dovecots     : %v.%u
#  tpop3d          : %Mf
#
# Note that Outlook 2003 seems to have problems with %v.%u format which was
# Dovecot's default, so if you're building a new server it would be a good
# idea to change this. %08Xu%08Xv should be pretty fail-safe.
#
# NOTE: Nowadays this is required to be set explicitly, since the old
# default was bad but it couldn't be changed without breaking existing
# installations. %08Xu%08Xv will be the new default, so use it for new
# installations.
#
pop3_uidl_format = %08Xu%08Xv

# POP3 logout format string:
#  %t - number of TOP commands
#  %p - number of bytes sent to client as a result of TOP command
#  %r - number of RETR commands
#  %b - number of bytes sent to client as a result of RETR command
#  %d - number of deleted messages
#  %m - number of messages (before deletion)
#  %s - mailbox size in bytes (before deletion)
#pop3_logout_format  =  top=%t/%p,  retr=%r/%b,  del=%d/%m, size=%s

# Support for dynamically loadable plugins. mail_plugins is a space separated
# list of plugins to load.
#mail_plugins =
mail_plugins = quota
#mail_plugin_dir = /usr/lib/dovecot/modules/pop3
```

```
  # Workarounds for various client bugs:
  #   outlook-no-nuls:
  #     Outlook and Outlook Express hang if mails contain NUL characters.
  #     This setting replaces them with 0x80 character.
  #   oe-ns-eoh:
  #     Outlook Express and Netscape Mail breaks if end of headers-line is
  #     missing. This option simply sends it if it's missing.
  # The list is space-separated.
  #pop3_client_workarounds =
}


##
## MANAGESIEVE specific settings
##

protocol managesieve {
  # Login executable location.
  #login_executable = /usr/libexec/dovecot/managesieve-login

  # MANAGESIEVE executable location. See IMAP's mail_executable
above for
  # examples how this could be changed.
  #mail_executable = /usr/libexec/dovecot/managesieve

  # Maximum MANAGESIEVE command line length in bytes. This
setting is
  # directly borrowed from IMAP. But, since long command lines are very
  # unlikely with MANAGESIEVE, changing this will not be very useful.
  #managesieve_max_line_length = 65536

  # Specifies the location of the symlink pointing to the active script in
  # the sieve storage directory. This must match the SIEVE setting used by
  # deliver (refer to http://wiki.dovecot.org/LDA/Sieve#location for more
  # info). Variable substitution with % is recognized.
  sieve=~/.dovecot.sieve

  # This specifies the path to the directory where the uploaded scripts must
  # be stored. In terms of '%' variable substitution it is identical to
  # dovecot's mail_location setting used by the mail protocol daemons.
  sieve_storage=~/sieve

  # If, for some inobvious reason, the sieve_storage remains unset, the
```

managesieve daemon uses the specification of the mail_location to find out
where to store the sieve files (see explaination in README.managesieve).
The example below, when uncommented, overrides any global mail_location
specification and stores all the scripts in '~/mail/sieve' if sieve_storage
is unset. However, you should always use the sieve_storage setting.
mail_location = mbox:~/mail

To fool managesieve clients that are focused on timesieved you can
specify the IMPLEMENTATION capability that the dovecot reports to clients
(default: dovecot).
#managesieve_implementation_string = Cyrus timsieved v2.2.13
}

##
LDA specific settings
##

protocol lda {
  # Address to use when sending rejection mails.
    # OTHER LOG PATH IS OUT OF THESE {}
  log_path = /var/vmail/dovecot-deliver.log
  postmaster_address = aestudio@aestudio.sytes.net

  # Hostname to use in various parts of sent mails, eg. in Message-Id.
  # Default is the system's real hostname.
  #hostname =

  # Support for dynamically loadable plugins. mail_plugins is a space separated
  # list of plugins to load.
  #mail_plugins =
  mail_plugins = quota
  #mail_plugin_dir = /usr/lib/dovecot/modules/lda

  # Binary to use for sending mails.
  #sendmail_path = /usr/lib/sendmail

  # UNIX socket path to master authentication server to find users.
  auth_socket_path = /var/run/dovecot/auth-master

```
  # Enabling Sieve plugin for server-side mail filtering
  mail_plugins = cmusieve
}
```

```
##
## Authentication processes
##
```

```
# Executable location
#auth_executable = /usr/lib/dovecot/dovecot-auth
```

```
# Set max. process size in megabytes.
#auth_process_size = 256
```

```
# Authentication cache size in kilobytes. 0 means it's disabled.
# Note that bsdauth, PAM and vpopmail require cache_key to be set for
caching
# to be used.
#auth_cache_size = 0
# Time to live in seconds for cached data. After this many seconds the
cached
# record is no longer used, *except* if the main database lookup returns
# internal failure. We also try to handle password changes automatically: If
# user's previous authentication was successful, but this one wasn't, the
# cache isn't used. For now this works only with plaintext authentication.
#auth_cache_ttl = 3600
```

```
# Space separated list of realms for SASL authentication mechanisms that
need
# them. You can leave it empty if you don't want to support multiple
realms.
# Many clients simply use the first one listed here, so keep the default realm
# first.
#auth_realms =
```

```
# Default realm/domain to use if none was specified. This is used for both
# SASL realms and appending @domain to username in plaintext logins.
#auth_default_realm =
```

```
# List of allowed characters in username. If the user-given username
contains
# a character not listed in here, the login automatically fails. This is just
```

an extra check to make sure user can't exploit any potential quote escaping
vulnerabilities with SQL/LDAP databases. If you want to allow all characters,
set this value to empty.
#auth_username_chars   =
abcdefghijklmnopqrstuvwxyzABCDEFGHIJKLMNOPQRSTUVWXYZ0
1234567890.-_@

Username character translations before it's looked up from databases. The
value contains series of from -> to characters. For example "#@/@" means
that '#' and '/' characters are translated to '@'.
#auth_username_translation =

Username formatting before it's looked up from databases. You can use
the standard variables here, eg. %Lu would lowercase the username, %n would
drop away the domain if it was given, or "%n-AT-%d" would change the '@' into
"-AT-". This translation is done after auth_username_translation changes.
#auth_username_format =

If you want to allow master users to log in by specifying the master
username within the normal username string (ie. not using SASL mechanism's
support for it), you can specify the separator character here. The format
is then <username><separator><master username>. UW-IMAP uses "*" as the
separator, so that could be a good choice.
#auth_master_user_separator =

Username to use for users logging in with ANONYMOUS SASL mechanism
#auth_anonymous_username = anonymous

More verbose logging. Useful for figuring out why authentication isn't
working.
#auth_verbose = no

Even more verbose logging for debugging purposes. Shows for example

SQL
queries.
#auth_debug = no

In case of password mismatches, log the passwords and used scheme so the
problem can be debugged. Requires auth_debug=yes to be set.
#auth_debug_passwords = no

Maximum number of dovecot-auth worker processes. They're used to execute
blocking passdb and userdb queries (eg. MySQL and PAM). They're
automatically created and destroyed as needed.
#auth_worker_max_count = 30

Host name to use in GSSAPI principal names. The default is to use the
name returned by gethostname().
#auth_gssapi_hostname =

Kerberos keytab to use for the GSSAPI mechanism. Will use the system
default (usually /etc/krb5.keytab) if not specified.
#auth_krb5_keytab =

auth default {
  # Space separated list of wanted authentication mechanisms:
  #   plain login digest-md5 cram-md5 ntlm rpa apop anonymous gssapi
  # NOTE: See also disable_plaintext_auth setting.
  mechanisms = plain login

  #
  # Password database is used to verify user's password (and nothing more).
  # You can have multiple passdbs and userdbs. This is useful if you want to
  # allow both system users (/etc/passwd) and virtual users to login without
  # duplicating the system users into virtual database.
  #
  # <doc/wiki/PasswordDatabase.txt>
  #
  # By adding master=yes setting inside a passdb you make the passdb a list
  # of "master users", who can log in as anyone else. Unless you're using PAM,
  # you probably still want the destination user to be looked up from passdb

that it really exists. This can be done by adding pass=yes setting to the
master passdb. <doc/wiki/Authentication.MasterUsers.txt>

Users can be temporarily disabled by adding a passdb with deny=yes.
If the user is found from that database, authentication will fail.
The deny passdb should always be specified before others, so it gets
checked first. Here's an example:

```
#passdb passwd-file {
  # File contains a list of usernames, one per line
  #args = /etc/dovecot.deny
  #deny = yes
#}
```

PAM authentication. Preferred nowadays by most systems.
Note that PAM can only be used to verify if user's password is correct,
so it can't be used as userdb. If you don't want to use a separate user
database (passwd usually), you can use static userdb.
REMEMBER: You'll need /etc/pam.d/dovecot file created for PAM
authentication   to   actually   work.
<doc/wiki/PasswordDatabase.PAM.txt>
  #passdb pam {
  # [blocking=yes] [session=yes] [setcred=yes]
  # [cache_key=<key>] [<service name>]
  #
  # By default a new process is forked from dovecot-auth for each PAM
lookup.
  # Setting blocking=yes uses the alternative way: dovecot-auth worker
  # processes do the PAM lookups.
  #
  # session=yes makes Dovecot open and immediately close PAM session.
Some
  # PAM plugins need this to work, such as pam_mkhomedir.
  #
  # setcred=yes makes Dovecot establish PAM credentials if some PAM
plugins
  # need that. They aren't ever deleted though, so this isn't enabled by
  # default.
  #
  # cache_key can be used to enable authentication caching for PAM
  # (auth_cache_size also needs to be set). It isn't enabled by default
  # because PAM modules can do all kinds of checks besides checking
password,

such as checking IP address. Dovecot can't know about these checks
without some help. cache_key is simply a list of variables (see
/usr/share/doc/dovecot-common/wiki/Variables.txt)   which   must
match for
the cached data to be used. Here are some examples:
%u - Username must match. Probably sufficient for most uses.
%u%r - Username and remote IP address must match.
%u%s - Username and service (ie. IMAP, POP3) must match.
#
If service name is "*", it means the authenticating service name
is used, eg. pop3 or imap (/etc/pam.d/pop3, /etc/pam.d/imap).
#
Some examples:
args = session=yes *
args = cache_key=%u dovecot
#args = dovecot
#}

System users (NSS, /etc/passwd, or similiar)
In many systems nowadays this uses Name Service Switch, which is
configured   in   /etc/nsswitch.conf.
<doc/wiki/AuthDatabase.Passwd.txt>
#passdb passwd {
  # [blocking=yes] - See userdb passwd for explanation
  #args =
#}

Shadow passwords for system users (NSS, /etc/shadow or similiar).
Deprecated by PAM nowadays.
<doc/wiki/PasswordDatabase.Shadow.txt>
#passdb shadow {
  # [blocking=yes] - See userdb passwd for explanation
  #args =
#}

PAM-like authentication for OpenBSD.
<doc/wiki/PasswordDatabase.BSDAuth.txt>
#passdb bsdauth {
  # [cache_key=<key>] - See cache_key in PAM for explanation.
  #args =
#}

passwd-like file with specified location

```
# <doc/wiki/AuthDatabase.PasswdFile.txt>
#passdb passwd-file {
  # Path for passwd-file
  #args =
#}


# checkpassword executable authentication
# NOTE: You will probably want to use "userdb prefetch" with this.
# <doc/wiki/PasswordDatabase.CheckPassword.txt>
#passdb checkpassword {
  # Path for checkpassword binary
  #args =
#}


# SQL database <doc/wiki/AuthDatabase.SQL.txt>
passdb sql {
  # Path for SQL configuration file
  args = /etc/dovecot/dovecot-sql.conf
}


# LDAP database <doc/wiki/AuthDatabase.LDAP.txt>
#passdb ldap {
  # Path for LDAP configuration file
  #args = /etc/dovecot/dovecot-ldap.conf
#}


# vpopmail authentication <doc/wiki/AuthDatabase.VPopMail.txt>
#passdb vpopmail {
  # [cache_key=<key>] - See cache_key in PAM for explanation.
  #args =
#}


#
# User database specifies where mails are located and what user/group
IDs
# own them. For single-UID configuration use "static".
#
# <doc/wiki/UserDatabase.txt>
#


# System users (NSS, /etc/passwd, or similiar). In many systems
nowadays this
# uses Name Service Switch, which is configured in /etc/nsswitch.conf.
```

```
# <doc/wiki/AuthDatabase.Passwd.txt>
userdb passwd {
  # [blocking=yes] - By default the lookups are done in the main dovecot-
auth
  # process. This setting causes the lookups to be done in auth worker
  # proceses. Useful with remote NSS lookups that may block.
  # NOTE: Be sure to use this setting with nss_ldap or users might get
  # logged in as each others!
  #args =
}

# passwd-like file with specified location
# <doc/wiki/AuthDatabase.PasswdFile.txt>
#userdb passwd-file {
  # Path for passwd-file
  #args =
#}

#        static       settings       generated        from       template
<doc/wiki/UserDatabase.Static.txt>
  #userdb static {
    # Template for the fields. Can return anything a userdb could normally
    # return. For example:
    #
    #  args = uid=500 gid=500 home=/var/mail/%u
    #
    # If you use deliver, it needs to look up users only from the userdb. This
    # of course doesn't work with static because there is no list of users.
    # Normally static userdb handles this by doing a passdb lookup. This
works
    # with most passdbs, with PAM being the most notable exception. If
you do
    # the user verification another way, you can add allow_all_users=yes to
    # the args in which case the passdb lookup is skipped.
    #
    #   args    =   uid=5050    gid=5050    home=/var/vmail/%d/%n
allow_all_users=yes
  # }

  # SQL database <doc/wiki/AuthDatabase.SQL.txt>
  userdb sql {
    # Path for SQL configuration file
    args = /etc/dovecot/dovecot-sql.conf
```

```
}

# LDAP database <doc/wiki/AuthDatabase.LDAP.txt>
#userdb ldap {
  # Path for LDAP configuration file
  #args = /etc/dovecot/dovecot-ldap.conf
#}

# vpopmail <doc/wiki/AuthDatabase.VPopMail.txt>
#userdb vpopmail {
#}

# "prefetch" user database means that the passdb already provided the
# needed information and there's no need to do a separate userdb lookup.
# This can be made to work with SQL and LDAP databases, see their
example
# configuration files for more information how to do it.
# <doc/wiki/UserDatabase.Prefetch.txt>
#userdb prefetch {
#}

# User to use for the process. This user needs access to only user and
# password databases, nothing else. Only shadow and pam authentication
# requires roots, so use something else if possible. Note that passwd
# authentication with BSDs internally accesses shadow files, which also
# requires roots. Note that this user is NOT used to access mails.
# That user is specified by userdb above.
user = root

# Directory where to chroot the process. Most authentication backends
don't
# work if this is set, and there's no point chrooting if auth_user is root.
# Note that valid_chroot_dirs isn't needed to use this setting.
#chroot =

# Number of authentication processes to create
#count = 1

# Require a valid SSL client certificate or the authentication fails.
#ssl_require_client_cert = no

# Take the username from client's SSL certificate, using
# X509_NAME_get_text_by_NID() which returns the subject's DN's
```

```
# CommonName.
#ssl_username_from_cert = no

# It's possible to export the authentication interface to other programs:
socket listen {
  master {
    # Master socket provides access to userdb information. It's typically
    # used to give Dovecot's local delivery agent access to userdb so it
    # can find mailbox locations.
    path = /var/run/dovecot/auth-master
    mode = 0600
    # Default user/group is the one who started dovecot-auth (root)
    user = vmail
    #group =
  }
  client {
    # The client socket is generally safe to export to everyone. Typical use
    # is to export it to your SMTP server so it can do SMTP AUTH
lookups
    # using it.
    path = /var/spool/postfix/private/auth
    mode = 0660
    user = postfix
    group = postfix
  }
}

## dovecot-lda specific settings
##
# socket listen {
#   master {
#     path = /var/run/dovecot/auth-master
#     mode = 0600
#     user = mail # User running Dovecot LDA
#       #group = mail # Or alternatively mode 0660 + LDA user in this
group
#   }
# }

}

# If you wish to use another authentication server than dovecot-auth, you
can
```

```
# use connect sockets. They are assumed to be already running, Dovecot's
master
# process only tries to connect to them. They don't need any other settings
# than the path for the master socket, as the configuration is done
elsewhere.
# Note that the client sockets must exist in the login_dir.
#auth external {
#  socket connect {
#    master {
#      path = /var/run/dovecot/auth-master
#    }
#  }
#}

##
## Dictionary server settings
##

# Dictionary can be used by some plugins to store key=value lists.
# Currently this is only used by dict quota backend. The dictionary can be
# used either directly or though a dictionary server. The following dict
block
# maps dictionary names to URIs when the server is used. These can then
be
# referenced using URIs in format "proxy:<name>".

dict {
  #quota = mysql:/etc/dovecot-dict-quota.conf
}

##
## Plugin settings
##

plugin {
  # Here you can give some extra environment variables to mail processes.
  # This is mostly meant for passing parameters to plugins. %variable
  # expansion is done for all values.

  # Quota plugin. Multiple backends are supported:
  #   dirsize: Find and sum all the files found from mail directory.
  #           Extremely SLOW with Maildir. It'll eat your CPU and disk I/O.
  #   dict: Keep quota stored in dictionary (eg. SQL)
```

```
#   maildir: Maildir++ quota
#   fs: Read-only support for filesystem quota
#quota = maildir
quota = maildir:storage=1000000:messages=1000
```

```
# ACL plugin. vfile backend reads ACLs from "dovecot-acl" file from
maildir
# directory. You can also optionally give a global ACL directory path
where
# ACLs are applied to all users' mailboxes. The global ACL directory
contains
# one file for each mailbox, eg. INBOX or sub.mailbox.
#acl = vfile:/etc/dovecot-acls
```

```
# Convert plugin. If set, specifies the source storage path which is
# converted to destination storage (mail_location) when the user logs in.
# The existing mail directory is renamed to <dir>-converted.
#convert_mail = mbox:%h/mail
# Skip mailboxes which we can't open successfully instead of aborting.
#convert_skip_broken_mailboxes = no
```

```
# Trash plugin. When saving a message would make user go over quota,
this
# plugin automatically deletes the oldest mails from configured mailboxes
# until the message can be saved within quota limits. The configuration
file
# is a text file where each line is in format: <priority> <mailbox name>
# Mails are first deleted in lowest -> highest priority number order
#trash = /etc/dovecot-trash.conf
```

```
# Lazy expunge plugin. Currently works only with maildirs. When a user
# expunges mails, the mails are moved to a mailbox in another namespace
# (1st). When a mailbox is deleted, the mailbox is moved to another
namespace
# (2nd) as well. Also if the deleted mailbox had any expunged messages,
# they're moved to a 3rd namespace. The mails won't be counted in
quota,
# and they're not deleted automatically (use a cronjob or something).
#lazy_expunge        =        .EXPUNGED/        .DELETED/
.DELETED/.EXPUNGED/
# New lines -- Esteban herrera
sieve_global_path = /var/vmail/globalsieverc
# End of new lines
```

}

```
/* ----------------------------
      /etc/fail2ban/jail.conf
----------------------------- */
# Fail2Ban configuration file.
#
# This file was composed for Debian systems from the original one
#  provided now under /usr/share/doc/fail2ban/examples/jail.conf
#  for additional examples.
#
# To avoid merges during upgrades DO NOT MODIFY THIS FILE
# and rather provide your changes in /etc/fail2ban/jail.local
#
# Author: Yaroslav O. Halchenko <debian@onerussian.com>
#
# $Revision: 281 $
#


# The DEFAULT allows a global definition of the options. They can be override
# in each jail afterwards.

[DEFAULT]

# "ignoreip" can be an IP address, a CIDR mask or a DNS host
ignoreip = 127.0.0.1
bantime  = 600
maxretry = 3


# "backend" specifies the backend used to get files modification. Available
# options are "gamin", "polling" and "auto".
# yoh: For some reason Debian shipped python-gamin didn't work as
expected
#     This issue left ToDo, so polling is default backend for now
backend = polling


#
# Destination email address used solely for the interpolations in
# jail.{conf,local} configuration files.
destemail = root@localhost


#
```

```
# ACTIONS
#

# Default banning action (e.g. iptables, iptables-new,
# iptables-multiport, shorewall, etc) It is used to define
# action_* variables. Can be overriden globally or per
# section within jail.local file
banaction = iptables-multiport

# email action. Since 0.8.1 upstream fail2ban uses sendmail
# MTA for the mailing. Change mta configuration parameter to mail
# if you want to revert to conventional 'mail'.
mta = sendmail

# Default protocol
protocol = tcp

#
# Action shortcuts. To be used to define action parameter

# The simplest action to take: ban only
action_    =    %(banaction)s[name=%(__name__)s,    port="%(port)s",
protocol="%(protocol)s]

# ban & send an e-mail with whois report to the destemail.
action_mw  =   %(banaction)s[name=%(__name__)s,   port="%(port)s",
protocol="%(protocol)s]
          %(mta)s-whois[name=%(__name__)s,         dest="%(destemail)s",
protocol="%(protocol)s]

# ban & send an e-mail with whois report and relevant log lines
# to the destemail.
action_mwl  =   %(banaction)s[name=%(__name__)s,   port="%(port)s",
protocol="%(protocol)s]
          %(mta)s-whois-lines[name=%(__name__)s,
dest="%(destemail)s", logpath=%(logpath)s]

# Choose default action.  To change, just override value of 'action' with the
# interpolation to the chosen action shortcut (e.g.  action_mw, action_mwl,
etc) in jail.local
# globally (section [DEFAULT]) or per specific section
action = %(action_)s
```

```
#
# JAILS
#

# Next jails corresponds to the standard configuration in Fail2ban 0.6
which
# was shipped in Debian. Enable any defined here jail by including
#
# [SECTION_NAME]
# enabled = true

#
# in /etc/fail2ban/jail.local.
#
# Optionally you may override any other parameter (e.g. banaction,
# action, port, logpath, etc) in that section within jail.local

[ssh]

enabled = true
port = ssh
filter = sshd
logpath  = /var/log/auth.log
maxretry = 6

# Generic filter for pam. Has to be used with action which bans all ports
# such as iptables-allports, shorewall
[pam-generic]

enabled = false
# pam-generic filter can be customized to monitor specific subset of 'tty's
filter = pam-generic
# port actually must be irrelevant but lets leave it all for some possible uses
port = all
banaction = iptables-allports
port     = anyport
logpath  = /var/log/auth.log
maxretry = 6

[xinetd-fail]

enabled   = false
filter    = xinetd-fail
```

```
port     = all
banaction = iptables-multiport-log
logpath  = /var/log/daemon.log
maxretry  = 2


[ssh-ddos]

enabled = false
port    = ssh
filter  = sshd-ddos
logpath  = /var/log/auth.log
maxretry = 6


#
# HTTP servers
#

[apache]

enabled = false
port = http,https
filter = apache-auth
logpath = /var/log/apache*/*error.log
maxretry = 6

# default action is now multiport, so apache-multiport jail was left
# for compatibility with previous (<0.7.6-2) releases
[apache-multiport]

enabled   = false
port   = http,https
filter   = apache-auth
logpath   = /var/log/apache*/*error.log
maxretry  = 6

[apache-noscript]

enabled = false
port    = http,https
filter  = apache-noscript
logpath = /var/log/apache*/*error.log
maxretry = 6
```

[apache-overflows]

enabled = false
port   = http,https
filter = apache-overflows
logpath = /var/log/apache*/*error.log
maxretry = 2

#
FTP servers
#

[vsftpd]

enabled = false
port = ftp,ftp-data,ftps,ftps-data
filter   = vsftpd
logpath = /var/log/vsftpd.log
# or overwrite it in jails.local to be
# logpath = /var/log/auth.log
# if you want to rely on PAM failed login attempts
# vsftpd's failregex should match both of those formats
maxretry = 6

[proftpd]

enabled = false
port = ftp,ftp-data,ftps,ftps-data
filter   = proftpd
logpath = /var/log/proftpd/proftpd.log
maxretry = 6

[wuftpd]

enabled = false
port = ftp,ftp-data,ftps,ftps-data
filter   = wuftpd
logpath = /var/log/auth.log
maxretry = 6

```
#
# Mail servers
#

[postfix]

enabled  = false
port  = smtp,ssmtp
filter   = postfix
logpath  = /var/log/mail.log


[couriersmtp]

enabled  = false
port  = smtp,ssmtp
filter   = couriersmtp
logpath  = /var/log/mail.log


#
# Mail servers authenticators: might be used for smtp,ftp,imap servers, so
# all relevant ports get banned
#

[courierauth]

enabled  = false
port  = smtp,ssmtp,imap2,imap3,imaps,pop3,pop3s
filter   = courierlogin
logpath  = /var/log/mail.log


[sasl]

enabled  = false
port  = smtp,ssmtp,imap2,imap3,imaps,pop3,pop3s
filter   = sasl
# You might consider monitoring /var/log/warn.log instead
# if you are running postfix. See http://bugs.debian.org/507990
logpath  = /var/log/mail.log
```

DNS Servers

```
# These jails block attacks against named (bind9). By default, logging is off
# with bind9 installation. You will need something like this:
#
# logging {
#    channel security_file {
#       file "/var/log/named/security.log" versions 3 size 30m;
#       severity dynamic;
#       print-time yes;
#    };
#    category security {
#       security_file;
#    };
# };
#
# in your named.conf to provide proper logging

# !!! WARNING !!!
#   Since UDP is connectionless protocol, spoofing of IP and immitation
#   of illegal actions is way too simple. Thus enabling of this filter
#   might provide an easy way for implementing a DoS against a chosen
#   victim. See
#   http://nion.modprobe.de/blog/archives/690-fail2ban-+-dns-fail.html
#   Please DO NOT USE this jail unless you know what you are doing.
#[named-refused-udp]
#
#enabled = false
#port    = domain,953
#protocol = udp
#filter  = named-refused
#logpath = /var/log/named/security.log

[named-refused-tcp]

enabled = false
port    = domain,953
protocol = tcp
filter  = named-refused
logpath = /var/log/named/security.log
```

```
/* -------------------------------------
      /etc/logrotate.d/dovecot-deliver
-------------------------------------- */
```

Nota: Este es el único archivo de logs para logrote que se ha creado manualmente, pero al final del proyecto los siguientes archivos se encuentran adicionalmente en el directorio /etc/logrotate/: apache2, apt, aptitude, clamav-daemon, clamav-freshclam, dpkg, exim4-base, exim4-paniclog, fail2ban, mysql-server, vsftpd. Se debe revisar para cada programa que instalamos si genera logs, donde los genera, si los podemos centralizar en /var/log/ a como lo hemos hecho durante todo el proyecto LE SF y estar al tanto de su crecimiento para crear o modificar una entrada con logrotate para comprimirlos y rotarlos. En ciertos casos como los logs de Apache2 se debe tener cuidado de no rotar logs en la medida de lo posible porque son usados para obtener datos estadísticos de las visitas en las webs y logrotate trata los grupos de logs como una serpiente que se muerde la cola, sobre-escribiendo el primer archivo del grupo cuando se llega al final del último en rotación. Se debe notar que el crecimiento de logs de servidor se disminuye al tener un Cluster de servidores en máxima disponibilidad (HA) ya que las peticiones de los clientes y sus logs se distribuyen entre todos los servidores de la granja. En ese caso la información estadística debe recuperarse de distintos puntos a como se explica en los videos de los DVDs del cluster de Linux Enterprise Sci-Fi.

```
/var/vmail/dovecot-deliver.log {
weekly
rotate 14
compress
}


/* -------------------------------------
      /etc/mysql/DISABLEDndb_mgmd.cnf
-------------------------------------- */
```

Nota: Este archivo es una configuración básica de MySQL Cluster 5.0. Queda pendiente agregarle la línea para especificar el directorio, partición o disco de BACKUP de las bases de datos, a como se explica en los DVD de Cluster de Linux Enterprise Sci Fi. Para la versión de este archivo de MySQL Cluster 7.2 se puede consultar también la documentación oficial de Oracle® MySQL Cluster.

```
[ndb_mgmd]
hostname=192.168.1.200
datadir=/home/my_cluster/ndb_data
NodeId=1

[ndbd default]
```

```
noofreplicas=2
DataMemory=128M
IndexMemory=64M
datadir=/home/my_cluster/ndb_data

[ndbd]
hostname=192.168.1.200
NodeId=3

[ndbd]
hostname=192.168.1.205
NodeId=4

[mysqld]
hostname=192.168.1.200
NodeId=50

/* ----------------------
        /etc/mysql/my.cnf
----------------------- */
#
# The MySQL database server configuration file.
#
# You can copy this to one of:
# - "/etc/mysql/my.cnf" to set global options,
# - "~/.my.cnf" to set user-specific options.
#
# One can use all long options that the program supports.
# Run program with --help to get a list of available options and with
# --print-defaults to see which it would actually understand and use.
#
# For explanations see
# http://dev.mysql.com/doc/mysql/en/server-system-variables.html


# This will be passed to all mysql clients
# It has been reported that passwords should be enclosed with ticks/quotes
# escpecially if they contain "#" chars...
# Remember to edit /etc/mysql/debian.cnf when changing the socket
location.
[client]
port        = 3306
socket          = /var/run/mysqld/mysqld.sock
```

```
# Here is entries for some specific programs
# The following values assume you have at least 32M ram

# This was formally known as [safe_mysqld]. Both versions are currently
parsed.
[mysqld_safe]
socket          = /var/run/mysqld/mysqld.sock
nice        = 0

[mysqld]
#
# * Basic Settings
#
user        = mysql
pid-file    = /var/run/mysqld/mysqld.pid
socket          = /var/run/mysqld/mysqld.sock
port        = 3306
basedir         = /usr
datadir         = /var/lib/mysql
tmpdir          = /tmp
language = /usr/share/mysql/english
skip-external-locking
#
# Instead of skip-networking the default is now to listen only on
# localhost which is more compatible and is not less secure.
#bind-address        = 127.0.0.1
bind-address         = 0.0.0.0
#
# * Fine Tuning
#
key_buffer          = 16M
max_allowed_packet      = 16M
thread_stack        = 192K
thread_cache_size       = 8
# This replaces the startup script and checks MyISAM tables if needed
# the first time they are touched
myisam-recover          = BACKUP
#max_connections         = 100
#table_cache         = 64
#thread_concurrency      = 10
#
# * Query Cache Configuration
#
```

```
query_cache_limit   = 1M
query_cache_size       = 16M
#
# * Logging and Replication
#
# Both location gets rotated by the cronjob.
# Be aware that this log type is a performance killer.
# As of 5.1 you can enable the log at runtime!
#general_log_file      = /var/log/mysql/mysql.log
#general_log        = 1
#
#      Error      logging      goes      to      syslog      due      to
/etc/mysql/conf.d/mysqld_safe_syslog.cnf.
#
# Here you can see queries with especially long duration
#log_slow_queries  = /var/log/mysql/mysql-slow.log
#long_query_time = 2
#log-queries-not-using-indexes
#
# The following can be used as easy to replay backup logs or for
replication.
# note: if you are setting up a replication slave, see README.Debian
about
#      other settings you may need to change.
#server-id          = 1
#log_bin           = /var/log/mysql/mysql-bin.log
expire_logs_days    = 10
max_binlog_size      = 100M
#binlog_do_db            = include_database_name
#binlog_ignore_db = include_database_name
#
# * InnoDB
#
# InnoDB is enabled by default with a 10MB datafile in /var/lib/mysql/.
# Read the manual for more InnoDB related options. There are many!
#
# * Security Features
#
# Read the manual, too, if you want chroot!
# chroot = /var/lib/mysql/
#
# For generating SSL certificates I recommend the OpenSSL GUI "tinyca".
#
```

```
# ssl-ca=/etc/mysql/cacert.pem
# ssl-cert=/etc/mysql/server-cert.pem
# ssl-key=/etc/mysql/server-key.pem

# --== Esteban edition on: 01-11-13 ==--
default_table_type = NDBCLUSTER
ndbcluster
ndb-connectstring=192.168.1.200

[mysql_cluster]
ndb-connectstring=192.168.1.200

[mysqldump]
quick
quote-names
max_allowed_packet      = 16M

[mysql]
#no-auto-rehash     # faster start of mysql but no tab completition

[isamchk]
key_buffer          = 16M

#
# * IMPORTANT: Additional settings that can override those from this
file!
#   The files must end with '.cnf', otherwise they'll be ignored.
#
!includedir /etc/mysql/conf.d/

/* ---------------------------
      /etc/network/interfaces
----------------------------- */
# This file describes the network interfaces available on your system
# and how to activate them. For more information, see interfaces(5).

# The loopback network interface
auto lo
iface lo inet loopback

# The primary network interface
#allow-hotplug eth0
#iface eth0 inet static
```

```
#address 192.168.1.205
#broadcast 192.168.1.255
#netmask 255.255.255.0
#gateway 192.168.1.1
#nameserver 192.168.1.1

allow-hotplug eth1
iface eth1 inet static
address 192.168.1.206
broadcast 192.168.1.255
netmask 255.255.255.0
gateway 192.168.1.1
nameserver 192.168.1.1

allow-hotplug eth2
iface eth2 inet static
address 192.168.1.207
broadcast 192.168.1.255
netmask 255.255.255.0
gateway 192.168.1.1
nameserver 192.168.1.1

allow-hotplug eth3
iface eth3 inet static
address 192.168.1.208
broadcast 192.168.1.255
netmask 255.255.255.0
gateway 192.168.1.1
nameserver 192.168.1.1

allow-hotplug eth4
iface eth4 inet static
address 192.168.1.209
broadcast 192.168.1.255
netmask 255.255.255.0
gateway 192.168.1.1
nameserver 192.168.1.1

# Next is the creation of the bridge interface
auto br0
iface br0 inet static

        address 192.168.1.205
```

```
        netmask 255.255.255.0
        broadcast 192.168.1.255
        gateway 192.168.1.1
        # dns-* options are implemented by resolvconf
        # package, if installed
        #dns-nameservers 193.168.1.1
        #dns-search sytes.net

        pre-up /usr/sbin/tunctl -u xcapncrunchx -t tap0
        pre-up ifconfig tap0 up
        #bridge_ports all tap0
        bridge_ports eth0
        bridge_maxwait 0
        post-down ifconfig tap0
        post-down tunctl -d tap0
```

/* -------------------------------
       /etc/network/interfacesBAK
-------------------------------- */
This file describes the network interfaces available on your system
and how to activate them. For more information, see interfaces(5).

The loopback network interface
auto lo
iface lo inet loopback

The primary network interface
allow-hotplug eth0
iface eth0 inet dhcp

/* -----------------------------
       /etc/php5/apache2/php.ini
------------------------------- */
[PHP]

::::::::::::
;;;;;;;;;;;;
; WARNING ;
::::::::::::
;;;;;;;;;;;;
; This is the default settings file for new PHP installations.
; By default, PHP installs itself with a configuration suitable for
; development purposes, and *NOT* for production purposes.
; For several security-oriented considerations that should be taken
; before going online with your site, please consult php.ini-recommended

; and http://php.net/manual/en/security.php.

;;;;;;;;;;;;;;;;;;;;
; About php.ini   ;
;;;;;;;;;;;;;;;;;;;;
; This file controls many aspects of PHP's behavior. In order for PHP to
; read it, it must be named 'php.ini'. PHP looks for it in the current
; working directory, in the path designated by the environment variable
; PHPRC, and in the path that was defined in compile time (in that order).
; Under Windows, the compile-time path is the Windows directory. The
; path in which the php.ini file is looked for can be overridden using
; the -c argument in command line mode.
;
; The syntax of the file is extremely simple. Whitespace and Lines
; beginning with a semicolon are silently ignored (as you probably guessed).
; Section headers (e.g. [Foo]) are also silently ignored, even though
; they might mean something in the future.
;
; Directives are specified using the following syntax:
; directive = value
; Directive names are *case sensitive* - foo=bar is different from
FOO=bar.
;
; The value can be a string, a number, a PHP constant (e.g. E_ALL or
M_PI), one
; of the INI constants (On, Off, True, False, Yes, No and None) or an
expression
; (e.g. E_ALL & ~E_NOTICE), or a quoted string ("foo").
;
; Expressions in the INI file are limited to bitwise operators and
parentheses:
; | bitwise OR
; &   bitwise AND
; ~   bitwise NOT
; !   boolean NOT
;
; Boolean flags can be turned on using the values 1, On, True or Yes.
; They can be turned off using the values 0, Off, False or No.
;
; An empty string can be denoted by simply not writing anything after the
equal
; sign, or by using the None keyword:

```
;
; foo =        ; sets foo to an empty string
; foo = none    ; sets foo to an empty string
; foo = "none" ; sets foo to the string 'none'
;
; If you use constants in your value, and these constants belong to a
; dynamically loaded extension (either a PHP extension or a Zend
extension),
; you may only use these constants *after* the line that loads the extension.
;
;
;;;;;;;;;;;;;;;;;;;;
; About this file ;
;;;;;;;;;;;;;;;;;;;;
; All the values in the php.ini-dist file correspond to the builtin
; defaults (that is, if no php.ini is used, or if you delete these lines,
; the builtin defaults will be identical).


;;;;;;;;;;;;;;;;;;;;;;;
; Language Options ;
;;;;;;;;;;;;;;;;;;;;;;;

; Enable the PHP scripting language engine under Apache.
engine = On

; Enable compatibility mode with Zend Engine 1 (PHP 4.x)
zend.ze1_compatibility_mode = Off

; Allow the <? tag.  Otherwise, only <?php and <script> tags are
recognized.
; NOTE: Using short tags should be avoided when developing applications
or
; libraries that are meant for redistribution, or deployment on PHP
; servers which are not under your control, because short tags may not
; be supported on the target server. For portable, redistributable code,
; be sure not to use short tags.
short_open_tag = On

; Allow ASP-style <% %> tags.
asp_tags = Off

; The number of significant digits displayed in floating point numbers.
```

precision   = 12

; Enforce year 2000 compliance (will cause problems with non-compliant browsers)
y2k_compliance = On

; Output buffering allows you to send header lines (including cookies) even
; after you send body content, at the price of slowing PHP's output layer a
; bit. You can enable output buffering during runtime by calling the output
; buffering functions. You can also enable output buffering for all files by
; setting this directive to On. If you wish to limit the size of the buffer
; to a certain size - you can use a maximum number of bytes instead of 'On',
as
; a value for this directive (e.g., output_buffering=4096).
output_buffering = Off

; You can redirect all of the output of your scripts to a function. For
; example, if you set output_handler to "mb_output_handler", character
; encoding will be transparently converted to the specified encoding.
; Setting any output handler automatically turns on output buffering.
; Note: People who wrote portable scripts should not depend on this ini
;   directive. Instead, explicitly set the output handler using ob_start().
;   Using this ini directive may cause problems unless you know what
script
;   is doing.
;   Note: You   cannot   use   both   "mb_output_handler"   with
"ob_iconv_handler"
;   and   you   cannot   use   both   "ob_gzhandler"   and
"zlib.output_compression".
; Note: output_handler must be empty if this is set 'On' !!!!
;   Instead you must use zlib.output_handler.
;output_handler =

; Transparent output compression using the zlib library
; Valid values for this option are 'off', 'on', or a specific buffer size
; to be used for compression (default is 4KB)
; Note: Resulting chunk size may vary due to nature of compression. PHP
;   outputs chunks that are few hundreds bytes each as a result of
;   compression. If you prefer a larger chunk size for better
;   performance, enable output_buffering in addition.
; Note: You need to use zlib.output_handler instead of the standard
;   output_handler, or otherwise the output will be corrupted.
zlib.output_compression = Off

;zlib.output_compression_level = -1

; You cannot specify additional output handlers if zlib.output_compression
; is activated here. This setting does the same as output_handler but in
; a different order.
;zlib.output_handler =

; Implicit flush tells PHP to tell the output layer to flush itself
; automatically after every output block. This is equivalent to calling the
; PHP function flush() after each and every call to print() or echo() and each
; and every HTML block. Turning this option on has serious performance
; implications and is generally recommended for debugging purposes only.
implicit_flush = Off

; The unserialize callback function will be called (with the undefined class'
; name as parameter), if the unserializer finds an undefined class
; which should be instantiated.
; A warning appears if the specified function is not defined, or if the
; function doesn't include/implement the missing class.
; So only set this entry, if you really want to implement such a
; callback-function.
unserialize_callback_func=

; When floats & doubles are serialized store serialize_precision significant
; digits after the floating point. The default value ensures that when floats
; are decoded with unserialize, the data will remain the same.
serialize_precision = 100

; Whether to enable the ability to force arguments to be passed by reference
; at function call time. This method is deprecated and is likely to be
; unsupported in future versions of PHP/Zend. The encouraged method of
; specifying which arguments should be passed by reference is in the function
; declaration. You're encouraged to try and turn this option Off and make
; sure your scripts work properly with it in order to ensure they will work
; with future versions of the language (you will receive a warning each time
; you use this feature, and the argument will be passed by value instead of by
; reference).
allow_call_time_pass_reference = On

;

```
; Safe Mode
;
; NOTE: this is considered a "broken" security measure.
;      Applications relying on this feature will not recieve full
;      support by the security team.  For more information please
;      see /usr/share/doc/php5-common/README.Debian.security
;
;safe_mode = Off

; By default, Safe Mode does a UID compare check when
; opening files. If you want to relax this to a GID compare,
; then turn on safe_mode_gid.
safe_mode_gid = Off

; When safe_mode is on, UID/GID checks are bypassed when
; including files from this directory and its subdirectories.
; (directory must also be in include_path or full path must
; be used when including)
;safe_mode_include_dir =

;   When   safe_mode   is   on,   only   executables   located   in   the
safe_mode_exec_dir
; will be allowed to be executed via the exec family of functions.
;safe_mode_exec_dir =


; Setting certain environment variables may be a potential security breach.
; This directive contains a comma-delimited list of prefixes.  In Safe Mode,
; the user may only alter environment variables whose names begin with the
; prefixes supplied here.  By default, users will only be able to set
; environment variables that begin with PHP_ (e.g. PHP_FOO=BAR).
;
; Note:  If this directive is empty, PHP will let the user modify ANY
; environment variable!
safe_mode_allowed_env_vars = PHP_

; This directive contains a comma-delimited list of environment variables
that
; the end user won't be able to change using putenv(). These variables will
be
; protected even if safe_mode_allowed_env_vars is set to allow to change
them.
safe_mode_protected_env_vars = LD_LIBRARY_PATH
```

; open_basedir, if set, limits all file operations to the defined directory
; and below. This directive makes most sense if used in a per-directory
; or per-virtualhost web server configuration file. This directive is
; *NOT* affected by whether Safe Mode is turned On or Off.

; NOTE: this is considered a "broken" security measure.
;   Applications relying on this feature will not recieve full
;   support by the security team. For more information please
;   see /usr/share/doc/php5-common/README.Debian.security
;

;open_basedir =
;open_basedir = /var/www

; This directive allows you to disable certain functions for security reasons.
; It receives a comma-delimited list of function names. This directive is
; *NOT* affected by whether Safe Mode is turned On or Off.
disable_functions =

; This directive allows you to disable certain classes for security reasons.
; It receives a comma-delimited list of class names. This directive is
; *NOT* affected by whether Safe Mode is turned On or Off.
disable_classes =

; Colors for Syntax Highlighting mode. Anything that's acceptable in
; <span style="color: ???????"> would work.
;highlight.string = #DD0000
;highlight.comment = #FF9900
;highlight.keyword = #007700
;highlight.bg   = #FFFFFF
;highlight.default = #0000BB
;highlight.html   = #000000

; If enabled, the request will be allowed to complete even if the user aborts
; the request. Consider enabling it if executing long request, which may end up
; being interrupted by the user or a browser timing out.
; ignore_user_abort = On

; Determines the size of the realpath cache to be used by PHP. This value should

```
; be increased on systems where PHP opens many files to reflect the
quantity of
; the file operations performed.
; realpath_cache_size=16k

; Duration of time, in seconds for which to cache realpath information for a
given
; file or directory. For systems with rarely changing files, consider increasing
this
; value.
; realpath_cache_ttl=120

;
; Misc
;
; Decides whether PHP may expose the fact that it is installed on the server
; (e.g. by adding its signature to the Web server header).  It is no security
; threat in any way, but it makes it possible to determine whether you use
PHP
; on your server or not.
;expose_php = On
; <new line security reaons!>
expose_php = Off

;;;;;;;;;;;;;;;;;;;;;
; Resource Limits ;
;;;;;;;;;;;;;;;;;;;;;

max_execution_time = 30     ; Maximum execution time of each script, in
seconds
max_input_time = 60 ; Maximum amount of time each script may spend
parsing request data
;max_input_nesting_level = 64 ; Maximum input variable nesting level
memory_limit = 128M       ; Maximum amount of memory a script may
consume (128MB)

;;;;;;;;;;;;;;;;;;;;;;;;;;;;;;;;
; Error handling and logging ;
;;;;;;;;;;;;;;;;;;;;;;;;;;;;;;;;

; error_reporting is a bit-field.  Or each number up to get desired error
; reporting level
```

; E_ALL   - All errors and warnings (doesn't include E_STRICT)
; E_ERROR   - fatal run-time errors
; E_RECOVERABLE_ERROR - almost fatal run-time errors
; E_WARNING   - run-time warnings (non-fatal errors)
; E_PARSE   - compile-time parse errors
; E_NOTICE   - run-time notices (these are warnings which often result
;   from a bug in your code, but it's possible that it was
;   intentional (e.g., using an uninitialized variable and
;   relying on the fact it's automatically initialized to an
;   empty string)
; E_STRICT   - run-time notices, enable to have PHP suggest changes
;   to your code which will ensure the best interoperability
;   and forward compatibility of your code
; E_CORE_ERROR   - fatal errors that occur during PHP's initial startup
; E_CORE_WARNING   - warnings (non-fatal errors) that occur during PHP's
;   initial startup
; E_COMPILE_ERROR   - fatal compile-time errors
; E_COMPILE_WARNING - compile-time warnings (non-fatal errors)
; E_USER_ERROR   - user-generated error message
; E_USER_WARNING   - user-generated warning message
; E_USER_NOTICE   - user-generated notice message
;
; Examples:
;
;   - Show all errors, except for notices and coding standards warnings
;
;error_reporting = E_ALL & ~E_NOTICE
;
;   - Show all errors, except for notices
;
;error_reporting = E_ALL & ~E_NOTICE | E_STRICT
;
;   - Show only errors
;
;error_reporting   =
E_COMPILE_ERROR|E_RECOVERABLE_ERROR|E_ERROR|E_C
ORE_ERROR
;
;   - Show all errors except for notices and coding standards warnings
;
error_reporting = E_ALL & ~E_NOTICE

```
; Print out errors (as a part of the output).  For production web sites,
; you're strongly encouraged to turn this feature off, and use error logging
; instead (see below).  Keeping display_errors enabled on a production web
site
; may reveal security information to end users, such as file paths on your
Web
; server, your database schema or other information.
;
; possible values for display_errors:
;
; Off      - Do not display any errors
; stderr    - Display errors to STDERR (affects only CGI/CLI binaries!)
;
;display_errors = "stderr"
;
; stdout (On) - Display errors to STDOUT
;
display_errors = Off

; Even when display_errors is on, errors that occur during PHP's startup
; sequence are not displayed.  It's strongly recommended to keep
; display_startup_errors off, except for when debugging.
display_startup_errors = Off

; Log errors into a log file (server-specific log, stderr, or error_log (below))
; As stated above, you're strongly advised to use error logging in place of
; error displaying on production web sites.
;log_errors = Off
log_errors = On

; Set maximum length of log_errors. In error_log information about the
source is
; added. The default is 1024 and 0 allows to not apply any maximum length
at all.
log_errors_max_len = 1024

; Do not log repeated messages. Repeated errors must occur in same file on
same
; line until ignore_repeated_source is set true.
ignore_repeated_errors = Off

; Ignore source of message when ignoring repeated messages. When this
```

setting
; is On you will not log errors with repeated messages from different files or
; source lines.
ignore_repeated_source = Off

; If this parameter is set to Off, then memory leaks will not be shown (on
; stdout or in the log). This has only effect in a debug compile, and if
; error reporting includes E_WARNING in the allowed list
report_memleaks = On

;report_zend_debug = 0

; Store the last error/warning message in $php_errormsg (boolean).
track_errors = Off

; Disable the inclusion of HTML tags in error messages.
; Note: Never use this feature for production boxes.
;html_errors = Off

; If html_errors is set On PHP produces clickable error messages that direct
; to a page describing the error or function causing the error in detail.
;   You   can   download   a   copy   of   the   PHP   manual   from
http://www.php.net/docs.php
; and change docref_root to the base URL of your local copy including the
; leading '/'. You must also specify the file extension being used including
; the dot.
; Note: Never use this feature for production boxes.
;docref_root = "/phpmanual/"
;docref_ext = .html

; String to output before an error message.
;error_prepend_string = "<font color=#ff0000>"

; String to output after an error message.
;error_append_string = "</font>"

; Log errors to specified file.
;error_log = filename

; Log errors to syslog (Event Log on NT, not valid in Windows 95).
;error_log = syslog

```
;;;;;;;;;;;;;;;;;;;
;;;;;;;;;;;;;;;;;;;;;
; Data Handling ;
;;;;;;;;;;;;;;;;;;;
;
; Note - track_vars is ALWAYS enabled as of PHP 4.0.3

; The separator used in PHP generated URLs to separate arguments.
; Default is "&".
;arg_separator.output = "&amp;"

; List of separator(s) used by PHP to parse input URLs into variables.
; Default is "&".
; NOTE: Every character in this directive is considered as separator!
;arg_separator.input = ";&"
```

; This directive describes the order in which PHP registers GET, POST, Cookie,
; Environment and Built-in variables (G, P, C, E & S respectively, often
; referred to as EGPCS or GPC). Registration is done from left to right, newer
; values override older values.
variables_order = "EGPCS"

; Whether or not to register the EGPCS variables as global variables. You may
; want to turn this off if you don't want to clutter your scripts' global scope
; with user data. This makes most sense when coupled with track_vars - in which
; case you can access all of the GPC variables through the $HTTP_*_VARS[],
; variables.
;
; You should do your best to write your scripts so that they do not require
; register_globals to be on; Using form variables as globals can easily lead
; to possible security problems, if the code is not very well thought of.

; NOTE: applications relying on this feature will not recieve full
;   support by the security team. For more information please
;   see /usr/share/doc/php5-common/README.Debian.security
;
register_globals = Off

; Whether or not to register the old-style input arrays, HTTP_GET_VARS

; and friends. If you're not using them, it's recommended to turn them off,
; for performance reasons.
register_long_arrays = On

; This directive tells PHP whether to declare the argv&argc variables (that
; would contain the GET information). If you don't use these variables, you
; should turn it off for increased performance.
register_argc_argv = On

; When enabled, the SERVER and ENV variables are created when they're first
; used (Just In Time) instead of when the script starts. If these variables
; are not used within a script, having this directive on will result in a
;   performance   gain.   The   PHP   directives   register_globals, register_long_arrays,
; and register_argc_argv must be disabled for this directive to have any affect.
auto_globals_jit = On

; Maximum size of POST data that PHP will accept.
post_max_size = 8M

; Magic quotes
;

; Magic quotes for incoming GET/POST/Cookie data.
magic_quotes_gpc = On

; Magic quotes for runtime-generated data, e.g. data from SQL, from exec(), etc.
magic_quotes_runtime = Off

; Use Sybase-style magic quotes (escape ' with " instead of \').
magic_quotes_sybase = Off

; Automatically add files before or after any PHP document.
auto_prepend_file =
auto_append_file =

; As of 4.0b4, PHP always outputs a character encoding by default in
; the Content-type: header. To disable sending of the charset, simply
; set it to be empty.

```
;
; PHP's built-in default is text/html
default_mimetype = "text/html"
;default_charset = "iso-8859-1"

; Always populate the $HTTP_RAW_POST_DATA variable.
;always_populate_raw_post_data = On


;;;;;;;;;;;;;;;;;;;;;;;;;;;
; Paths and Directories ;
;;;;;;;;;;;;;;;;;;;;;;;;;;;

; UNIX: "/path1:/path2"
;include_path = ".:/usr/share/php"
include_path                                              =
".:/home/aestudio/public_html:/home/aestudio/include:/home/aestudio
/include/classes"
;
; Windows: "\path1;\path2"
;include_path = ".;c:\php\includes"

; The root of the PHP pages, used only if nonempty.
; if PHP was not compiled with FORCE_REDIRECT, you SHOULD set
doc_root
; if you are running php as a CGI under any web server (other than IIS)
; see documentation for security issues.  The alternate is to use the
; cgi.force_redirect configuration below
doc_root =

; The directory under which PHP opens the script using /~username used
only
; if nonempty.
user_dir =

; Directory in which the loadable extensions (modules) reside.
; extension_dir = "./"

; Whether or not to enable the dl() function.  The dl() function does NOT
work
; properly in multithreaded servers, such as IIS or Zeus, and is automatically
; disabled on them.
; NOTE: this is a potential security hole and is disabled by default in debian
```

enable_dl = Off

; cgi.force_redirect is necessary to provide security running PHP as a CGI under
; most web servers. Left undefined, PHP turns this on by default. You can
; turn it off here AT YOUR OWN RISK
; **You CAN safely turn this off for IIS, in fact, you MUST.**
; cgi.force_redirect = 1

; if cgi.nph is enabled it will force cgi to always sent Status: 200 with
; every request.
; cgi.nph = 1

; if cgi.force_redirect is turned on, and you are not running under Apache or Netscape
; (iPlanet) web servers, you MAY need to set an environment variable name that PHP
; will look for to know it is OK to continue execution. Setting this variable MAY
; cause security issues, KNOW WHAT YOU ARE DOING FIRST.
; cgi.redirect_status_env = ;

; cgi.fix_pathinfo provides *real* PATH_INFO/PATH_TRANSLATED support for CGI. PHP's
; previous behaviour was to set PATH_TRANSLATED to SCRIPT_FILENAME, and to not grok
; what PATH_INFO is. For more information on PATH_INFO, see the cgi specs. Setting
; this to 1 will cause PHP CGI to fix it's paths to conform to the spec. A setting
; of zero causes PHP to behave as before. Default is 1. You should fix your scripts
; to use SCRIPT_FILENAME rather than PATH_TRANSLATED.
; cgi.fix_pathinfo=0

; FastCGI under IIS (on WINNT based OS) supports the ability to impersonate
; security tokens of the calling client. This allows IIS to define the
; security context that the request runs under. mod_fastcgi under Apache
; does not currently support this feature (03/17/2002)
; Set to 1 if running under IIS. Default is zero.
; fastcgi.impersonate = 1;

```
; Disable logging through FastCGI connection
; fastcgi.logging = 0

; cgi.rfc2616_headers configuration option tells PHP what type of headers
to
; use when sending HTTP response code. If it's set 0 PHP sends Status:
header that
; is supported by Apache. When this option is set to 1 PHP will send
; RFC2616 compliant header.
; Default is zero.
;cgi.rfc2616_headers = 0


;;;;;;;;;;;;;;;;;;
; File Uploads ;
;;;;;;;;;;;;;;;;;;

; Whether to allow HTTP file uploads.
file_uploads = On

; Temporary directory for HTTP uploaded files (will use system default if
not
; specified).
;upload_tmp_dir =

; Maximum allowed size for uploaded files.
upload_max_filesize = 2M


; Maximum number of files that can be uploaded via a single request
max_file_uploads = 50

;;;;;;;;;;;;;;;;;;;;
; Fopen wrappers ;
;;;;;;;;;;;;;;;;;;;;

; Whether to allow the treatment of URLs (like http:// or ftp://) as files.
;allow_url_fopen = On


; Whether to allow include/require to open URLs (like http:// or ftp://) as
files.
allow_url_include = Off
```

; Define the anonymous ftp password (your email address)
;from="john@doe.com"

; Define the User-Agent string
; user_agent="PHP"

; Default timeout for socket based streams (seconds)
default_socket_timeout = 60

; If your scripts have to deal with files from Macintosh systems,
; or you are running on a Mac and need to deal with files from
; unix or win32 systems, setting this flag will cause PHP to
; automatically detect the EOL character in those files so that
; fgets() and file() will work regardless of the source of the file.
; auto_detect_line_endings = Off

;;;;;;;;;;;;;;;;;;;;;;;
; Dynamic Extensions ;
;;;;;;;;;;;;;;;;;;;;;;;
;
; If you wish to have an extension loaded automatically, use the following
; syntax:
;
;   extension=modulename.extension
;
; For example, on Windows:
;
;   extension=msql.dll
;
; ... or under UNIX:
;
;   extension=msql.so
;
; Note that it should be the name of the module only; no directory
information
; needs to go here. Specify the location of the extension with the
; extension_dir directive above.

;;;;;;;;;;;;;;;;;;;
; Module Settings ;

;;;;;;;;;;;;;;;;;;;;
;;;;;;;;;;;;;;;;;;;;;

[Date]
; Defines the default timezone used by the date functions
;date.timezone =

;date.default_latitude = 31.7667
;date.default_longitude = 35.2333

;date.sunrise_zenith = 90.583333
;date.sunset_zenith = 90.583333

[filter]
;filter.default = unsafe_raw
;filter.default_flags =

[iconv]
;iconv.input_encoding = ISO-8859-1
;iconv.internal_encoding = ISO-8859-1
;iconv.output_encoding = ISO-8859-1

[sqlite]
;sqlite.assoc_case = 0

[xmlrpc]
;xmlrpc_error_number = 0
;xmlrpc_errors = 0

[Pcre]
;PCRE library backtracking limit.
;pcre.backtrack_limit=100000

;PCRE library recursion limit.
;Please note that if you set this value to a high number you may consume all
;the available process stack and eventually crash PHP (due to reaching the
;stack size limit imposed by the Operating System).
;pcre.recursion_limit=100000

[Syslog]
; Whether or not to define the various syslog variables (e.g. $LOG_PID,
; $LOG_CRON, etc.). Turning it off is a good idea performance-wise. In
;   runtime,   you   can   define   these   variables   by   calling
define_syslog_variables().

define_syslog_variables = Off

[mail function]
; For Win32 only.
SMTP = localhost
smtp_port = 25

; For Win32 only.
;sendmail_from = me@example.com

; For Unix only. You may supply arguments as well (default: "sendmail -t -
i").
;sendmail_path =

; Force the addition of the specified parameters to be passed as extra
parameters
; to the sendmail binary. These parameters will always replace the value of
; the 5th parameter to mail(), even in safe mode.
;mail.force_extra_parameters =

[SQL]
sql.safe_mode = Off

[ODBC]
;odbc.default_db   = Not yet implemented
;odbc.default_user = Not yet implemented
;odbc.default_pw   = Not yet implemented

; Allow or prevent persistent links.
odbc.allow_persistent = On

; Check that a connection is still valid before reuse.
odbc.check_persistent = On

; Maximum number of persistent links. -1 means no limit.
odbc.max_persistent = -1

; Maximum number of links (persistent + non-persistent). -1 means no
limit.
odbc.max_links = -1

; Handling of LONG fields. Returns number of bytes to variables. 0
means

```
; passthru.
odbc.defaultlrl = 4096
```

```
; Handling of binary data.  0 means passthru, 1 return as is, 2 convert to
char.
; See the documentation on odbc_binmode and odbc_longreadlen for an
explanation
; of uodbc.defaultlrl and uodbc.defaultbinmode
odbc.defaultbinmode = 1
```

```
[MySQL]
; Allow or prevent persistent links.
mysql.allow_persistent = On
```

```
; Maximum number of persistent links.  -1 means no limit.
mysql.max_persistent = -1
```

```
; Maximum number of links (persistent + non-persistent).  -1 means no
limit.
mysql.max_links = -1
```

```
; Default port number for mysql_connect().  If unset, mysql_connect() will
use
; the $MYSQL_TCP_PORT or the mysql-tcp entry in /etc/services or the
; compile-time value defined MYSQL_PORT (in that order).  Win32 will
only look
; at MYSQL_PORT.
mysql.default_port =
```

```
; Default socket name for local MySQL connects.  If empty, uses the built-
in
; MySQL defaults.
mysql.default_socket =
```

```
; Default host for mysql_connect() (doesn't apply in safe mode).
mysql.default_host =
```

```
; Default user for mysql_connect() (doesn't apply in safe mode).
mysql.default_user =
```

```
; Default password for mysql_connect() (doesn't apply in safe mode).
; Note that this is generally a *bad* idea to store passwords in this file.
;    *Any*    user    with    PHP    access    can    run    'echo
```

get_cfg_var("mysql.default_password")
; and reveal this password! And of course, any users with read access to this
; file will be able to reveal the password as well.
mysql.default_password =

; Maximum time (in seconds) for connect timeout. -1 means no limit
mysql.connect_timeout = 60

; Trace mode. When trace_mode is active (=On), warnings for table/index
scans and
; SQL-Errors will be displayed.
mysql.trace_mode = Off

[MySQLi]

; Maximum number of links. -1 means no limit.
mysqli.max_links = -1

; Default port number for mysqli_connect(). If unset, mysqli_connect() will
use
; the $MYSQL_TCP_PORT or the mysql-tcp entry in /etc/services or the
; compile-time value defined MYSQL_PORT (in that order). Win32 will
only look
; at MYSQL_PORT.
mysqli.default_port = 3306

; Default socket name for local MySQL connects. If empty, uses the built-
in
; MySQL defaults.
mysqli.default_socket =

; Default host for mysql_connect() (doesn't apply in safe mode).
mysqli.default_host =

; Default user for mysql_connect() (doesn't apply in safe mode).
mysqli.default_user =

; Default password for mysqli_connect() (doesn't apply in safe mode).
; Note that this is generally a *bad* idea to store passwords in this file.
;   *Any*   user   with   PHP   access   can   run   'echo
get_cfg_var("mysqli.default_pw")
; and reveal this password! And of course, any users with read access to this
; file will be able to reveal the password as well.

mysqli.default_pw =

; Allow or prevent reconnect
mysqli.reconnect = Off

[mSQL]
; Allow or prevent persistent links.
msql.allow_persistent = On

; Maximum number of persistent links. -1 means no limit.
msql.max_persistent = -1

; Maximum number of links (persistent+non persistent). -1 means no limit.
msql.max_links = -1

[OCI8]
; enables privileged connections using external credentials
(OCI_SYSOPER, OCI_SYSDBA)
;oci8.privileged_connect = Off

; Connection: The maximum number of persistent OCI8 connections per
; process. Using -1 means no limit.
;oci8.max_persistent = -1

; Connection: The maximum number of seconds a process is allowed to
; maintain an idle persistent connection. Using -1 means idle
; persistent connections will be maintained forever.
;oci8.persistent_timeout = -1

; Connection: The number of seconds that must pass before issuing a
; ping during oci_pconnect() to check the connection validity. When
; set to 0, each oci_pconnect() will cause a ping. Using -1 disables
; pings completely.
;oci8.ping_interval = 60

; Tuning: This option enables statement caching, and specifies how
; many statements to cache. Using 0 disables statement caching.
;oci8.statement_cache_size = 20

; Tuning: Enables statement prefetching and sets the default number of
; rows that will be fetched automatically after statement execution.
;oci8.default_prefetch = 10

; Compatibility. Using On means oci_close() will not close
; oci_connect() and oci_new_connect() connections.
;oci8.old_oci_close_semantics = Off

[PostgresSQL]
; Allow or prevent persistent links.
pgsql.allow_persistent = On

; Detect broken persistent links always with pg_pconnect().
; Auto reset feature requires a little overheads.
pgsql.auto_reset_persistent = Off

; Maximum number of persistent links. -1 means no limit.
pgsql.max_persistent = -1

; Maximum number of links (persistent+non persistent). -1 means no limit.
pgsql.max_links = -1

; Ignore PostgreSQL backends Notice message or not.
; Notice message logging require a little overheads.
pgsql.ignore_notice = 0

; Log PostgreSQL backends Noitce message or not.
; Unless pgsql.ignore_notice=0, module cannot log notice message.
pgsql.log_notice = 0

[Sybase]
; Allow or prevent persistent links.
sybase.allow_persistent = On

; Maximum number of persistent links. -1 means no limit.
sybase.max_persistent = -1

; Maximum number of links (persistent + non-persistent). -1 means no
limit.
sybase.max_links = -1

;sybase.interface_file = "/usr/sybase/interfaces"

; Minimum error severity to display.
sybase.min_error_severity = 10

; Minimum message severity to display.

sybase.min_message_severity = 10

; Compatibility mode with old versions of PHP 3.0.
; If on, this will cause PHP to automatically assign types to results according
; to their Sybase type, instead of treating them all as strings. This
; compatibility mode will probably not stay around forever, so try applying
; whatever necessary changes to your code, and turn it off.
sybase.compatability_mode = Off

[Sybase-CT]
; Allow or prevent persistent links.
sybct.allow_persistent = On

; Maximum number of persistent links. -1 means no limit.
sybct.max_persistent = -1

; Maximum number of links (persistent + non-persistent). -1 means no
limit.
sybct.max_links = -1

; Minimum server message severity to display.
sybct.min_server_severity = 10

; Minimum client message severity to display.
sybct.min_client_severity = 10

[bcmath]
; Number of decimal digits for all bcmath functions.
bcmath.scale = 0

[browscap]
;browscap = extra/browscap.ini

[Informix]
; Default host for ifx_connect() (doesn't apply in safe mode).
ifx.default_host =

; Default user for ifx_connect() (doesn't apply in safe mode).
ifx.default_user =

; Default password for ifx_connect() (doesn't apply in safe mode).
ifx.default_password =

; Allow or prevent persistent links.
ifx.allow_persistent = On

; Maximum number of persistent links. -1 means no limit.
ifx.max_persistent = -1

; Maximum number of links (persistent + non-persistent). -1 means no limit.
ifx.max_links = -1

; If on, select statements return the contents of a text blob instead of its id.
ifx.textasvarchar = 0

; If on, select statements return the contents of a byte blob instead of its id.
ifx.byteasvarchar = 0

; Trailing blanks are stripped from fixed-length char columns. May help the
; life of Informix SE users.
ifx.charasvarchar = 0

; If on, the contents of text and byte blobs are dumped to a file instead of
; keeping them in memory.
ifx.blobinfile = 0

; NULL's are returned as empty strings, unless this is set to 1. In that case,
; NULL's are returned as string 'NULL'.
ifx.nullformat = 0

[Session]
; Handler used to store/retrieve data.
session.save_handler = files

; Argument passed to save_handler. In the case of files, this is the path
; where data files are stored. Note: Windows users have to change this
; variable in order to use PHP's session functions.
;
; As of PHP 4.0.1, you can define the path as:
;
;   session.save_path = "N;/path"
;
; where N is an integer. Instead of storing all the session files in
; /path, what this will do is use subdirectories N-levels deep, and
; store the session data in those directories. This is useful if you

```
; or your OS have problems with lots of files in one directory, and is
; a more efficient layout for servers that handle lots of sessions.
;
; NOTE 1: PHP will not create this directory structure automatically.
;        You can use the script in the ext/session dir for that purpose.
; NOTE 2: See the section on garbage collection below if you choose to
;        use subdirectories for session storage
;
; The file storage module creates files using mode 600 by default.
; You can change that by using
;
;    session.save_path = "N;MODE;/path"
;
; where MODE is the octal representation of the mode. Note that this
; does not overwrite the process's umask.
;session.save_path = /var/lib/php5

; Whether to use cookies.
session.use_cookies = 1

;session.cookie_secure =

; This option enables administrators to make their users invulnerable to
; attacks which involve passing session ids in URLs; defaults to 0.
; session.use_only_cookies = 1

; Name of the session (used as cookie name).
session.name = PHPSESSID

; Initialize session on request startup.
session.auto_start = 0

; Lifetime in seconds of cookie or, if 0, until browser is restarted.
session.cookie_lifetime = 0

; The path for which the cookie is valid.
session.cookie_path = /

; The domain for which the cookie is valid.
session.cookie_domain =

; Whether or not to add the httpOnly flag to the cookie, which makes it
inaccessible to browser scripting languages such as JavaScript.
```

session.cookie_httponly =

; Handler used to serialize data. php is the standard serializer of PHP.
session.serialize_handler = php

; Define the probability that the 'garbage collection' process is started
; on every session initialization.
; The probability is calculated by using gc_probability/gc_divisor,
; e.g. 1/100 means there is a 1% chance that the GC process starts
; on each request.

; This is disabled in the Debian packages, due to the strict permissions
; on /var/lib/php5. Instead of setting this here, see the cronjob at
; /etc/cron.d/php5, which uses the session.gc_maxlifetime setting below.
; php scripts using their own session.save_path should make sure garbage
; collection is enabled by setting session.gc_probability
;session.gc_probability = 0
session.gc_divisor   = 100

; After this number of seconds, stored data will be seen as 'garbage' and
; cleaned up by the garbage collection process.
session.gc_maxlifetime = 1440

; NOTE: If you are using the subdirectory option for storing session files
;   (see session.save_path above), then garbage collection does *not*
;   happen automatically. You will need to do your own garbage
;   collection through a shell script, cron entry, or some other method.
;   For example, the following script would is the equivalent of
;   setting session.gc_maxlifetime to 1440 (1440 seconds = 24 minutes):
;   cd /path/to/sessions; find -cmin +24 | xargs rm

; PHP 4.2 and less have an undocumented feature/bug that allows you to
; to initialize a session variable in the global scope, albeit register_globals
; is disabled. PHP 4.3 and later will warn you, if this feature is used.
; You can disable the feature and the warning separately. At this time,
; the warning is only displayed, if bug_compat_42 is enabled.

session.bug_compat_42 = 1
session.bug_compat_warn = 1

; Check HTTP Referer to invalidate externally stored URLs containing ids.
; HTTP_REFERER has to contain this substring for the session to be
; considered as valid.

session.referer_check =

; How many bytes to read from the file.
session.entropy_length = 0

; Specified here to create the session id.
session.entropy_file =

;session.entropy_length = 16

;session.entropy_file = /dev/urandom

; Set to {nocache,private,public,} to determine HTTP caching aspects
; or leave this empty to avoid sending anti-caching headers.
session.cache_limiter = nocache

; Document expires after n minutes.
session.cache_expire = 180

; trans sid support is disabled by default.
; Use of trans sid may risk your users security.
; Use this option with caution.
; - User may send URL contains active session ID
;   to other person via. email/irc/etc.
; - URL that contains active session ID may be stored
;   in publically accessible computer.
; - User may access your site with the same session ID
;   always using URL stored in browser's history or bookmarks.
session.use_trans_sid = 0

; Select a hash function
; 0: MD5   (128 bits)
; 1: SHA-1 (160 bits)
session.hash_function = 0

; Define how many bits are stored in each character when converting
; the binary hash data to something readable.
;
; 4 bits: 0-9, a-f
; 5 bits: 0-9, a-v
; 6 bits: 0-9, a-z, A-Z, "-", ","
session.hash_bits_per_character = 4

; The URL rewriter will look for URLs in a defined set of HTML tags.
; form/fieldset are special; if you include them here, the rewriter will
; add a hidden <input> field with the info which is otherwise appended
; to URLs. If you want XHTML conformity, remove the form entry.
; Note that all valid entries require a "=", even if no value follows.
url_rewriter.tags   =
"a=href,area=href,frame=src,input=src,form=,fieldset="

[MSSQL]
; Allow or prevent persistent links.
mssql.allow_persistent = On

; Maximum number of persistent links. -1 means no limit.
mssql.max_persistent = -1

; Maximum number of links (persistent+non persistent). -1 means no limit.
mssql.max_links = -1

; Minimum error severity to display.
mssql.min_error_severity = 10

; Minimum message severity to display.
mssql.min_message_severity = 10

; Compatibility mode with old versions of PHP 3.0.
mssql.compatability_mode = Off

; Connect timeout
;mssql.connect_timeout = 5

; Query timeout
;mssql.timeout = 60

; Valid range 0 - 2147483647. Default = 4096.
;mssql.textlimit = 4096

; Valid range 0 - 2147483647. Default = 4096.
;mssql.textsize = 4096

; Limits the number of records in each batch. 0 = all records in one batch.
;mssql.batchsize = 0

; Specify how datetime and datetim4 columns are returned

; On => Returns data converted to SQL server settings
; Off => Returns values as YYYY-MM-DD hh:mm:ss
;mssql.datetimeconvert = On

; Use NT authentication when connecting to the server
mssql.secure_connection = Off

; Specify max number of processes. -1 = library default
; msdlib defaults to 25
; FreeTDS defaults to 4096
;mssql.max_procs = -1

; Specify client character set.
; If empty or not set the client charset from freetds.comf is used
; This is only used when compiled with FreeTDS
;mssql.charset = "ISO-8859-1"

[Assertion]
; Assert(expr); active by default.
;assert.active = On

; Issue a PHP warning for each failed assertion.
;assert.warning = On

; Don't bail out by default.
;assert.bail = Off

; User-function to be called if an assertion fails.
;assert.callback = 0

; Eval the expression with current error_reporting(). Set to true if you want
; error_reporting(0) around the eval().
;assert.quiet_eval = 0

[COM]
; path to a file containing GUIDs, IIDs or filenames of files with TypeLibs
;com.typelib_file =
; allow Distributed-COM calls
;com.allow_dcom = true
; autoregister constants of a components typlib on com_load()
;com.autoregister_typelib = true
; register constants casesensitive
;com.autoregister_casesensitive = false

```
; show warnings on duplicate constant registrations
;com.autoregister_verbose = true

[mbstring]
; language for internal character representation.
;mbstring.language = Japanese

; internal/script encoding.
; Some encoding cannot work as internal encoding.
; (e.g. SJIS, BIG5, ISO-2022-*)
;mbstring.internal_encoding = EUC-JP

; http input encoding.
;mbstring.http_input = auto

; http output encoding. mb_output_handler must be
; registered as output buffer to function
;mbstring.http_output = SJIS

; enable automatic encoding translation according to
; mbstring.internal_encoding setting. Input chars are
; converted to internal encoding by setting this to On.
; Note: Do _not_ use automatic encoding translation for
;       portable libs/applications.
;mbstring.encoding_translation = Off

; automatic encoding detection order.
; auto means
;mbstring.detect_order = auto

; substitute_character used when character cannot be converted
; one from another
;mbstring.substitute_character = none;

; overload(replace) single byte functions by mbstring functions.
; mail(), ereg(), etc are overloaded by mb_send_mail(), mb_ereg(),
; etc. Possible values are 0,1,2,4 or combination of them.
; For example, 7 for overload everything.
; 0: No overload
; 1: Overload mail() function
; 2: Overload str*() functions
; 4: Overload ereg*() functions
;mbstring.func_overload = 0
```

[FrontBase]
;fbsql.allow_persistent = On
;fbsql.autocommit = On
;fbsql.show_timestamp_decimals = Off
;fbsql.default_database =
;fbsql.default_database_password =
;fbsql.default_host =
;fbsql.default_password =
;fbsql.default_user = "_SYSTEM"
;fbsql.generate_warnings = Off
;fbsql.max_connections = 128
;fbsql.max_links = 128
;fbsql.max_persistent = -1
;fbsql.max_results = 128

[gd]
; Tell the jpeg decode to libjpeg warnings and try to create
; a gd image. The warning will then be displayed as notices
; disabled by default
;gd.jpeg_ignore_warning = 0

[exif]
; Exif UNICODE user comments are handled as UCS-2BE/UCS-2LE and
JIS as JIS.
; With mbstring support this will automatically be converted into the
encoding
; given by corresponding encode setting. When empty
mbstring.internal_encoding
; is used. For the decode settings you can distinguish between motorola and
; intel byte order. A decode setting cannot be empty.
;exif.encode_unicode = ISO-8859-15
;exif.decode_unicode_motorola = UCS-2BE
;exif.decode_unicode_intel   = UCS-2LE
;exif.encode_jis =
;exif.decode_jis_motorola = JIS
;exif.decode_jis_intel   = JIS

[Tidy]
; The path to a default tidy configuration file to use when using tidy
;tidy.default_config = /usr/local/lib/php/default.tcfg

; Should tidy clean and repair output automatically?

; WARNING: Do not use this option if you are generating non-html content
; such as dynamic images
tidy.clean_output = Off

[soap]
; Enables or disables WSDL caching feature.
soap.wsdl_cache_enabled=1
; Sets the directory name where SOAP extension will put cache files.
soap.wsdl_cache_dir="/tmp"
; (time to live) Sets the number of second while cached file will be used
; instead of original one.
soap.wsdl_cache_ttl=86400

; Local Variables:
; tab-width: 4
; End:

/* -----------------------------------
      /etc/phpmyadmin/config.inc.php
------------------------------------- */
      Nota: Este archivo es posible editarlo para cambiar opciones como contraseñas, pero no se ha cambiado nada porque la instalación completa la cubren los programas APT y DPKG. Mejor no tocarlo y sino primero realizar una copia de respaldo.

/* ------------------------
      /etc/postfix/main.cf
-------------------------- */
See /usr/share/postfix/main.cf.dist for a commented, more complete version

Debian specific: Specifying a file name will cause the first
line of that file to be used as the name. The Debian default
is /etc/mailname.
#myorigin = /etc/mailname

smtpd_banner = $myhostname ESMTP $mail_name (Debian/GNU)
biff = no

# appending .domain is the MUA's job.
append_dot_mydomain = no

Uncomment the next line to generate "delayed mail" warnings
#delay_warning_time = 4h

readme_directory = no

# TLS parameters
smtpd_tls_cert_file=/etc/ssl/certs/ssl-cert-snakeoil.pem
smtpd_tls_key_file=/etc/ssl/private/ssl-cert-snakeoil.key
smtpd_use_tls=yes
smtpd_tls_session_cache_database   =
btree:${data_directory}/smtpd_scache
smtp_tls_session_cache_database = btree:${data_directory}/smtp_scache

See /usr/share/doc/postfix/TLS_README.gz in the postfix-doc package for
information on enabling SSL in the smtp client.

myhostname = aestudio.sytes.net
alias_maps = hash:/etc/aliases
alias_database = hash:/etc/aliases
myorigin = /etc/mailname
mydestination = localhost.sytes.net, , localhost
relayhost =
mynetworks = 127.0.0.0/8 [::ffff:127.0.0.0]/104 [::1]/128
#mynetworks = 192.168.1.0/24
#mynetworks =
mailbox_command = procmail -a "$EXTENSION"
mailbox_size_limit = 0
recipient_delimiter = +
inet_interfaces = all

--== New lines ==--
Virtual map files:
virtual_mailbox_domains   =   mysql:/etc/postfix/mysql-virtual-mailbox-domains.cf
virtual_uid_maps = static:5050
virtual_gid_maps = static:5050
virtual_mailbox_maps = mysql:/etc/postfix/mysql-virtual-mailbox-maps.cf
virtual_alias_maps   =   mysql:/etc/postfix/mysql-virtual-alias-maps.cf,mysql:/etc/postfix/mysql-email2email.cf
# Dovecot service:
virtual_transport = dovecot:

```
dovecot_destination_recipient_limit = 1
# Authenticated SMTP:
smtpd_sasl_type = dovecot
smtpd_sasl_path = private/auth
smtpd_sasl_auth_enable = yes
smtpd_recipient_restrictions                                    =
permit_mynetworks,permit_sasl_authenticated,reject_unauth_destination,
permit
smtpd_tls_auth_only=no
# Amavis service:
content_filter = smtp-amavis:[127.0.0.1]:10024
receive_override_options = no_address_mappings


/* --------------------------
     /etc/postfix/master.cf
---------------------------- */
#
# Postfix master process configuration file.  For details on the format
# of the file, see the master(5) manual page (command: "man 5 master").
#
# Do not forget to execute "postfix reload" after editing this file.
#
#
============================================
=============================
# service type  private unpriv  chroot  wakeup  maxproc command + args
#              (yes)  (yes)  (yes)  (never) (100)
#
============================================
=============================
smtp     inet n     -     -     -     -      smtpd
#submission inet n     -     -     -     -      smtpd
# -o smtpd_tls_security_level=encrypt
# -o smtpd_sasl_auth_enable=yes
# -o smtpd_client_restrictions=permit_sasl_authenticated,reject
# -o milter_macro_daemon_name=ORIGINATING
#smtps    inet n     -     -     -     -      smtpd
# -o smtpd_tls_wrappermode=yes
# -o smtpd_sasl_auth_enable=yes
# -o smtpd_client_restrictions=permit_sasl_authenticated,reject
# -o milter_macro_daemon_name=ORIGINATING
#628     inet n     -     -     -     -      qmqpd
pickup   fifo n     -     -     60    1      pickup
```

```
cleanup   unix n    -    -    -    0    cleanup
qmgr      fifo n    -    n    300  1    qmgr
#qmgr     fifo n    -    -    300  1    oqmgr
tlsmgr    unix -    -    -    1000? 1   tlsmgr
rewrite   unix -    -    -    -    -    trivial-rewrite
bounce    unix -    -    -    -    0    bounce
defer     unix -    -    -    -    0    bounce
trace     unix -    -    -    -    0    bounce
verify    unix -    -    -    -    1    verify
flush     unix n    -    -    1000? 0   flush
proxymap  unix -    -    n    -    -    proxymap
proxywrite unix -   -    n    -    1    proxymap
smtp      unix -    -    -    -    -    smtp
# When relaying mail as backup MX, disable fallback_relay to avoid MX
loops
relay     unix -    -    -    -    -    smtp
      -o smtp_fallback_relay=
#     -o smtp_helo_timeout=5 -o smtp_connect_timeout=5
showq     unix n    -    -    -    -    showq
error     unix -    -    -    -    -    error
retry     unix -    -    -    -    -    error
discard   unix -    -    -    -    -    discard
local     unix -    n    n    -    -    local
virtual   unix -    n    n    -    -    virtual
lmtp      unix -    -    -    -    -    lmtp
anvil     unix -    -    -    -    1    anvil
scache    unix -    -    -    -    1    scache
#
#
=================================================
==========================
# Interfaces to non-Postfix software. Be sure to examine the manual
# pages of the non-Postfix software to find out what options it wants.
#
# Many of the following services use the Postfix pipe(8) delivery
# agent.  See the pipe(8) man page for information about ${recipient}
# and other message envelope options.
#
=================================================
=========================
#
# maildrop. See the Postfix MAILDROP_README file for details.
# Also specify in main.cf: maildrop_destination_recipient_limit=1
```

```
#
maildrop  unix -   n   n    -  -    pipe
  flags=DRhu user=vmail argv=/usr/bin/maildrop -d ${recipient}
#
# See the Postfix UUCP_README file for configuration details.
#
uucp   unix -   n   n    -  -    pipe
  flags=Fqhu user=uucp argv=uux -r -n -z -a$sender - $nexthop!rmail
($recipient)
#
# Other external delivery methods.
#
ifmail  unix -   n   n    -  -    pipe
  flags=F user=ftn argv=/usr/lib/ifmail/ifmail -r $nexthop ($recipient)
bsmtp  unix -   n   n    -  -    pipe
  flags=Fq. user=bsmtp argv=/usr/lib/bsmtp/bsmtp -t$nexthop -f$sender
$recipient
scalemail-backend unix  -  n   n   -   2   pipe
  flags=R   user=scalemail   argv=/usr/lib/scalemail/bin/scalemail-store
${nexthop} ${user} ${extension}
mailman unix -   n   n    -  -    pipe
  flags=FR user=list argv=/usr/lib/mailman/bin/postfix-to-mailman.py
  ${nexthop} ${user}
dovecot unix -   n   n    -  -    pipe
  flags=DRhu   user=vmail:vmail   argv=/usr/lib/dovecot/deliver   -d
${recipient}
smtp-amavis unix -  -   n   -   2 smtp
   -o smtp_data_done_timeout=1200
   -o smtp_send_xforward_command=yes
   -o disable_dns_lookups=yes
   -o max_use=20
127.0.0.1:10025 inet n -    -   -    - smtpd
   -o content_filter=
   -o local_recipient_maps=
   -o relay_recipient_maps=
   -o smtpd_restriction_classes=
   -o smtpd_delay_reject=no
   -o smtpd_client_restrictions=permit_mynetworks,reject
   -o smtpd_helo_restrictions=
   -o smtpd_sender_restrictions=
   -o smtpd_recipient_restrictions=permit_mynetworks,reject
   -o smtpd_data_restrictions=reject_unauth_pipelining
   -o smtpd_end_of_data_restrictions=
```

-o mynetworks=127.0.0.0/8
-o smtpd_error_sleep_time=0
-o smtpd_soft_error_limit=1001
-o smtpd_hard_error_limit=1000
-o smtpd_client_connection_count_limit=0
-o smtpd_client_connection_rate_limit=0
-o
receive_override_options=no_header_body_checks,no_unknown_recipient
_checks
-o local_header_rewrite_clients=

/* -------------------------------
        /etc/spamassassin/local.cf
--------------------------------- */

Nota: Este archivo no se ha modificado y de acuerdo con nuestra configuración NO es el lugar correcto para configurar ciertos parámetros del Spamassassin como el nivel en el que un mensaje de correo es considerado spamming. De Spamassassin solo tomamos los filtros Bayesianos o reglas pero se aplican con AMaViS.

/* ------------------------
        /etc/ssh/sshd_config
------------------------- */
Package generated configuration file
See the sshd(8) manpage for details

What ports, IPs and protocols we listen for
#Port 49
Port 22
Use these options to restrict which interfaces/protocols sshd will bind to
#ListenAddress ::
#ListenAddress 0.0.0.0
Protocol 2
HostKeys for protocol version 2
HostKey /etc/ssh/ssh_host_rsa_key
HostKey /etc/ssh/ssh_host_dsa_key
#Privilege Separation is turned on for security
UsePrivilegeSeparation yes

Lifetime and size of ephemeral version 1 server key
KeyRegenerationInterval 3600
ServerKeyBits 768

```
# Logging
SyslogFacility AUTH
LogLevel INFO

# Authentication:
LoginGraceTime 120
PermitRootLogin yes
StrictModes yes

RSAAuthentication yes
PubkeyAuthentication yes
AuthorizedKeysFile %h/.ssh/authorized_keys

# Don't read the user's ~/.rhosts and ~/.shosts files
IgnoreRhosts yes
# For this to work you will also need host keys in /etc/ssh_known_hosts
RhostsRSAAuthentication no
# similar for protocol version 2
HostbasedAuthentication no
# Uncomment if you don't trust ~/.ssh/known_hosts for
RhostsRSAAuthentication
#IgnoreUserKnownHosts yes

# To enable empty passwords, change to yes (NOT RECOMMENDED)
PermitEmptyPasswords no

# Change to yes to enable challenge-response passwords (beware issues with
# some PAM modules and threads)
ChallengeResponseAuthentication no

# Change to no to disable tunnelled clear text passwords
#PasswordAuthentication yes

# Kerberos options
#KerberosAuthentication no
#KerberosGetAFSToken no
#KerberosOrLocalPasswd yes
#KerberosTicketCleanup yes

# GSSAPI options
#GSSAPIAuthentication no
#GSSAPICleanupCredentials yes
```

```
X11Forwarding yes
X11DisplayOffset 10
PrintMotd no
PrintLastLog yes
TCPKeepAlive yes
#UseLogin no

#MaxStartups 10:30:60
#Banner /etc/issue.net

# Allow client to pass locale environment variables
AcceptEnv LANG LC_*

Subsystem sftp /usr/lib/openssh/sftp-server

UsePAM yes

/* -----------------
      /etc/sudoers
------------------- */
# /etc/sudoers
#
# This file MUST be edited with the 'visudo' command as root.
#
# See the man page for details on how to write a sudoers file.
#

Defaults       env_reset

# Host alias specification

# User alias specification
User_Alias BACKUPER = xcapncrunchx

# Cmnd alias specification
Cmnd_Alias DEBAK = /usr/bin/rsync, /usr/bin/apt-get

#User priviledge specification
#Use this line like the grid to guide you
# User_Alias       Host_Alias  =(Runas_Alias)         Authentication
Cmnd_Alias
root        ALL=(ALL)                          ALL
```

BACKUPER   ALL=(ALL)   NOPASSWD: ALL

```
# Uncomment to allow members of group sudo to not need a password
# (Note that later entries override this, so you might need to move
# it further down)
# %sudo ALL=NOPASSWD: ALL
```

/* --------------------
    /etc/tripwire/
-------------------- */

Nota: Los archivos genéricos de este programa no han sido cambiados durante la creación de Linux Enterprise SF pero todas las políticas deben ser revisadas durante la instalación del servidor y antes de ponerlo en producción para hacer más efectivo y rápido el análisis postmorten de seguridad o para detectar archivos no deseados en el sistema como por ejemplo rootkits, troyanos u otro tipo de virus.

/* ---------------------------------
    /etc/webalizer/webalizer.conf
--------------------------------- */

Nota: No se han incluído todas las líneas del archivo debido a su extensión, pero sí hasta el punto donde se puedan ver todas las modificaciones hechas en DVD en el proyecto LE SF.

```
#
# Sample Webalizer configuration file
# Copyright 1997-2000 by Bradford L. Barrett (brad@mrunix.net)
#
# Distributed under the GNU General Public License.  See the
# files "Copyright" and "COPYING" provided with the webalizer
# distribution for additional information.
#
# This is a sample configuration file for the Webalizer (ver 2.01)
# Lines starting with pound signs '#' are comment lines and are
# ignored.  Blank lines are skipped as well.  Other lines are considered
# as configuration lines, and have the form "ConfigOption  Value" where
# ConfigOption is a valid configuration keyword, and Value is the value
# to assign that configuration option.  Invalid keyword/values are
# ignored, with appropriate warnings being displayed.  There must be
# at least one space or tab between the keyword and its value.
#
# As of version 0.98, The Webalizer will look for a 'default' configuration
# file named "webalizer.conf" in the current directory, and if not found
# there, will look for "/etc/webalizer.conf".
```

LogFile defines the web server log file to use. If not specified
here or on on the command line, input will default to STDIN. If
the log filename ends in '.gz' (ie: a gzip compressed file), it will
be decompressed on the fly as it is being read.

LogFile /var/log/apache2/access.log.1

LogType defines the log type being processed. Normally, the Webalizer
expects a CLF or Combined web server log as input. Using this option,
you can process ftp logs as well (xferlog as produced by wu-ftp and
others), or Squid native logs. Values can be 'clf', 'ftp' or 'squid',
with 'clf' the default.

#LogType   clf

OutputDir is where you want to put the output files. This should
should be a full path name, however relative ones might work as well.
If no output directory is specified, the current directory will be used.

OutputDir /var/www/webalizer

HistoryName allows you to specify the name of the history file produced
by the Webalizer. The history file keeps the data for up to 12 months
worth of logs, used for generating the main HTML page (index.html).
The default is a file named "webalizer.hist", stored in the specified
output directory. If you specify just the filename (without a path),
it will be kept in the specified output directory. Otherwise, the path
is relative to the output directory, unless absolute (leading /).

#HistoryName   webalizer.hist

Incremental processing allows multiple partial log files to be used
instead of one huge one. Useful for large sites that have to rotate
their log files more than once a month. The Webalizer will save its
internal state before exiting, and restore it the next time run, in
order to continue processing where it left off. This mode also causes
The Webalizer to scan for and ignore duplicate records (records already
processed by a previous run). See the README file for additional
information. The value may be 'yes' or 'no', with a default of 'no'.
The file 'webalizer.current' is used to store the current state data,
and is located in the output directory of the program (unless changed

\# with the IncrementalName option below). Please read at least the section
\# on Incremental processing in the README file before you enable this
option.

\#Incremental no

\# IncrementalName allows you to specify the filename for saving the
\# incremental data in. It is similar to the HistoryName option where the
\# name is relative to the specified output directory, unless an absolute
\# filename is specified. The default is a file named "webalizer.current"
\# kept in the normal output directory. If you don't specify "Incremental"
\# as 'yes' then this option has no meaning.

\#IncrementalName webalizer.current

\# ReportTitle is the text to display as the title. The hostname
\# (unless blank) is appended to the end of this string (seperated with
\# a space) to generate the final full title string.
\# Default is (for english) "Usage Statistics for".

ReportTitle Usage statistics for

\# HostName defines the hostname for the report. This is used in
\# the title, and is prepended to the URL table items. This allows
\# clicking on URL's in the report to go to the proper location in
\# the event you are running the report on a 'virtual' web server,
\# or for a server different than the one the report resides on.
\# If not specified here, or on the command line, webalizer will
\# try to get the hostname via a uname system call. If that fails,
\# it will default to "localhost".

HostName aestudio

\# HTMLExtension allows you to specify the filename extension to use
\# for generated HTML pages. Normally, this defaults to "html", but
\# can be changed for sites who need it (like for PHP embeded pages).

\#HTMLExtension html

\# PageType lets you tell the Webalizer what types of URL's you
\# consider a 'page'. Most people consider html and cgi documents
\# as pages, while not images and audio files. If no types are
\# specified, defaults will be used ('htm*', 'cgi' and HTMLExtension

if different for web logs, 'txt' for ftp logs).

PageType htm*
PageType cgi
#PageType   phtml
PageType php3
#PageType   pl
PageType php

PagePrefix allows all requests with a specified prefix to be
considered as 'pages'. If you want everything under /documents
to be treated as pages no matter what their extension is. Also
useful if you have cgi-scripts with PATH_INFO.
#PagePrefix /mycgi/parameters

UseHTTPS should be used if the analysis is being run on a
secure server, and links to urls should use 'https://' instead
of the default 'http://'. If you need this, set it to 'yes'.
Default is 'no'. This only changes the behaviour of the 'Top
URL's' table.

#UseHTTPS   no

DNSCache specifies the DNS cache filename to use for reverse DNS
lookups.
This file must be specified if you wish to perform name lookups on any
IP
addresses found in the log file. If an absolute path is not given as
part of the filename (ie: starts with a leading '/'), then the name is
relative to the default output directory. See the DNS.README file for
additional information.

#DNSCache   dns_cache.db

DNSChildren allows you to specify how many "children" processes are
run to perform DNS lookups to create or update the DNS cache file.
If a number is specified, the DNS cache file will be created/updated
each time the Webalizer is run, immediately prior to normal processing,
by running the specified number of "children" processes to perform
DNS lookups. If used, the DNS cache filename MUST be specified as
well. The default value is zero (0), which disables DNS cache file
creation/updates at run time. The number of children processes to
run may be anywhere from 1 to 100, however a large number may effect

normal system operations. Reasonable values should be between 5 and
20. See the DNS.README file for additional information.

#DNSChildren   0

HTMLPre defines HTML code to insert at the very beginning of the
file. Default is the DOCTYPE line shown below. Max line length
is 80 characters, so use multiple HTMLPre lines if you need more.

#HTMLPre <!DOCTYPE HTML PUBLIC "-//W3C//DTD HTML 4.0
Transitional//EN">

HTMLHead   defines   HTML   code   to   insert   within   the
<HEAD></HEAD>
block, immediately after the <TITLE> line. Maximum line length
is 80 characters, so use multiple lines if needed.

#HTMLHead <META NAME="author" CONTENT="The Webalizer">

HTMLBody defined the HTML code to be inserted, starting with the
<BODY> tag. If not specified, the default is shown below. If
used, you MUST include your own <BODY> tag as the first line.
Maximum line length is 80 char, use multiple lines if needed.

#HTMLBody   <BODY   BGCOLOR="#E8E8E8"   TEXT="#000000"
LINK="#0000FF" VLINK="#FF0000">

/* -----------------
     /etc/aliases
------------------- */
/etc/aliases
mailer-daemon: postmaster
postmaster: root
nobody: root
hostmaster: root
usenet: root
news: root
webmaster: root
www: root
ftp: root
abuse: root
noc: root
security: root

root: xcapncrunchx
clamav: root

```
/* -----------------
     /etc/crontab
------------------- */
# /etc/crontab: system-wide crontab
# Unlike any other crontab you don't have to run the `crontab'
# command to install the new version when you edit this file
# and files in /etc/cron.d. These files also have username fields,
# that none of the other crontabs do.

SHELL=/bin/sh
PATH=/usr/local/sbin:/usr/local/bin:/sbin:/bin:/usr/sbin:/usr/bin

# m h dom mon dow user      command
17 * * * * root   cd / && run-parts --report /etc/cron.hourly
25 6 * * * root test -x /usr/sbin/anacron || ( cd / && run-parts --report
/etc/cron.daily )
47 6 * * 7 root test -x /usr/sbin/anacron || ( cd / && run-parts --report
/etc/cron.weekly )
52 6 1 * * root test -x /usr/sbin/anacron || ( cd / && run-parts --report
/etc/cron.monthly )
#
# awstats for the virtual hosts
0 * * * * root sh /home/xcapncrunchx/awstats.sh
# wealizer for the virtual hosts
0 * * * * root sh /home/xcapncrunchx/webalizer.sh
# cluster hosts replication
*/4 * * * * root sh /etc/balance/Balance-push.sh
# Apache logs cluster replication
0 * * * * root sh /etc/init.d/apache-logs-replication.sh

/* ---------------
     /etc/fstab
----------------- */
# /etc/fstab: static file system information.
#
# <file system> <mount point>   <type> <options>        <dump>
<pass>
proc          /proc       proc    defaults    0    0
/dev/sda1     /           ext3    defaults,errors=remount-ro 0    1
/dev/sda9                 /home                                   ext3
```

```
usrjquota=aquota.user,grpjquota=aquota.group,jqfmt=vfsv0 0        1
/dev/sda8      /tmp          ext3    defaults      0      2
/dev/sda5      /usr          ext3    defaults      0      2
/dev/sda6                        /var                              ext3
usrjquota=aquota.user,grpjquota=aquota.group,jqfmt=vfsv0 0        1
/dev/sda7      none          swap    sw            0      0
/dev/hdc       /media/cdrom0   udf,iso9660 user,noauto    0      0
/dev/fd0       /media/floppy0  auto    rw,user,noauto  0      0
```

```
/* --------------------
     /etc/host.conf
--------------------- */
multi on
```

```
/* -------------------
     /etc/hostname
------------------- */
x2
```

```
/* ---------------
     /etc/hosts
----------------- */
127.0.0.1  localhost
127.0.1.1      x2.aestudio.sytes.net x2 mx2 mail2
#192.168.1.198   foobar.aestudio.sytes.net foobar
192.168.1.199  foobar.aestudio.asytes.net foobar

192.168.1.200   x1.aestudio.sytes.net x1 mx1 mail1
192.168.1.201   x1.aestudio.sytes.net x1 mx1 mail1
192.168.1.202   x1.aestudio.sytes.net x1 mx1 mail1
192.168.1.203   x1.aestudio.sytes.net x1 mx1 mail1
192.168.1.204   x1.aestudio.sytes.net x1 mx1 mail1
192.168.1.205   x2.aestudio.sytes.net x2 mx2 mail2
192.168.1.206   x2.aestudio.sytes.net x2 mx2 mail2
192.168.1.207   x2.aestudio.sytes.net x2 mx2 mail2
192.168.1.208   x2.aestudio.sytes.net x2 mx2 mail2
192.168.1.209   x2.aestudio.sytes.net x2 mx2 mail2


# The following lines are desirable for IPv6 capable hosts
::1    ip6-localhost ip6-loopback
fe00::0 ip6-localnet
ff00::0 ip6-mcastprefix
```

ff02::1 ip6-allnodes
ff02::2 ip6-allrouters
ff02::3 ip6-allhosts

/* ---------------------
    /etc/hosts.allow
---------------------- */
Nota: No se modifica este archivo durante el desarrollo de Linux Enterprise Sci-Fi, pero puede llegar a utilizarse como TCP Wrappers.
/etc/hosts.allow: list of hosts that are allowed to access the system.
See the manual pages hosts_access(5), hosts_options(5)
and /usr/doc/netbase/portmapper.txt.gz
#
Example: ALL: LOCAL @some_netgroup
ALL: .foobar.edu EXCEPT terminalserver.foobar.edu
#
If you're going to protect the portmapper use the name "portmap" for the
daemon name. Remember that you can only use the keyword "ALL" and IP
addresses (NOT host or domain names) for the portmapper, as well as for
rpc.mountd (the NFS mount daemon). See portmap(8), rpc.mountd(8) and
/usr/share/doc/portmap/portmapper.txt.gz for further information.
#

/* --------------------
    /etc/hosts.deny
---------------------- */
Nota: No se modifica este archivo durante el desarrollo de Linux Enterprise Sci-Fi, pero puede llegar a utilizarse como TCP Wrappers.
/etc/hosts.deny: list of hosts that are _not_ allowed to access the system.
See the manual pages hosts_access(5), hosts_options(5)
and /usr/doc/netbase/portmapper.txt.gz
#
Example: ALL: some.host.name, .some.domain
ALL EXCEPT in.fingerd: other.host.name, .other.domain
#
If you're going to protect the portmapper use the name "portmap" for the
daemon name. Remember that you can only use the keyword "ALL" and IP

addresses (NOT host or domain names) for the portmapper. See portmap(8)
and /usr/doc/portmap/portmapper.txt.gz for further information.
#
The PARANOID wildcard matches any host whose name does not match its
address.

You may wish to enable this to ensure any programs that don't
validate looked up hostnames still leave understandable logs. In past
versions of Debian this has been the default.
ALL: PARANOID

/* --------------------
      /etc/mailname
-------------------- */
aestudio.sytes.net

/* --------------
      /etc/mtab
---------------- */
/dev/sda1 / ext3 rw,errors=remount-ro 0 0
tmpfs /lib/init/rw tmpfs rw,nosuid,mode=0755 0 0
proc /proc proc rw,noexec,nosuid,nodev 0 0
sysfs /sys sysfs rw,noexec,nosuid,nodev 0 0
udev /dev tmpfs rw,mode=0755 0 0
tmpfs /dev/shm tmpfs rw,nosuid,nodev 0 0
devpts /dev/pts devpts rw,noexec,nosuid,gid=5,mode=620 0 0
/dev/sda9   /home   ext3
rw,usrjquota=aquota.user,grpjquota=aquota.group,jqfmt=vfsv0 0 0
/dev/sda8 /tmp ext3 rw 0 0
/dev/sda5 /usr ext3 rw 0 0
/dev/sda6   /var   ext3
rw,usrjquota=aquota.user,grpjquota=aquota.group,jqfmt=vfsv0 0 0

/* --------------------
      /etc/networks
-------------------- */
default   0.0.0.0
loopback 127.0.0.0
link-local 169.254.0.0

/* ------------------------

/etc/nsswitch.conf
------------------------ */
/etc/nsswitch.conf
#
Example configuration of GNU Name Service Switch functionality.
If you have the `glibc-doc-reference' and `info' packages installed, try:
`info libc "Name Service Switch"' for information about this file.

passwd: compat
group: compat
shadow: compat

hosts: files dns
networks: files

protocols: db files
services: db files
ethers: db files
rpc: db files

netgroup: nis

/* -------------------
     /etc/ntp.conf
--------------------- */
/etc/ntp.conf, configuration for ntpd; see ntp.conf(5) for help

driftfile /var/lib/ntp/ntp.drift

Enable this if you want statistics to be logged.
statsdir /var/log/ntpstats/

statistics loopstats peerstats clockstats
filegen loopstats file loopstats type day enable
filegen peerstats file peerstats type day enable
filegen clockstats file clockstats type day enable

You do need to talk to an NTP server or two (or three).
#server ntp.your-provider.example

pool.ntp.org maps to about 1000 low-stratum NTP servers. Your server

will
pick a different set every time it starts up. Please consider joining the
pool: <http://www.pool.ntp.org/join.html>
server 0.debian.pool.ntp.org iburst
server 1.debian.pool.ntp.org iburst
server 2.debian.pool.ntp.org iburst
server 3.debian.pool.ntp.org iburst

Access control configuration; see /usr/share/doc/ntp-doc/html/accopt.html for
details. The web page <http://support.ntp.org/bin/view/Support/AccessRestrictions>
might also be helpful.
#
Note that "restrict" applies to both servers and clients, so a configuration
that might be intended to block requests from certain clients could also end
up blocking replies from your own upstream servers.

By default, exchange time with everybody, but don't allow configuration.
restrict -4 default kod notrap nomodify nopeer noquery
restrict -6 default kod notrap nomodify nopeer noquery

Local users may interrogate the ntp server more closely.
restrict 127.0.0.1
restrict ::1

Clients from this (example!) subnet have unlimited access, but only if
cryptographically authenticated.
#restrict 192.168.123.0 mask 255.255.255.0 notrust

If you want to provide time to your local subnet, change the next line.
(Again, the address is an example only.)
#broadcast 192.168.123.255

If you want to listen to time broadcasts on your local subnet, de-comment the
next lines. Please do this only if you trust everybody on the network!
#disable auth
#broadcastclient

```
/* -----------------
      /etc/passwd
----------------- */
root:x:0:0:root:/root:/bin/bash
daemon:x:1:1:daemon:/usr/sbin:/bin/sh
bin:x:2:2:bin:/bin:/bin/sh
sys:x:3:3:sys:/dev:/bin/sh
sync:x:4:65534:sync:/bin:/bin/sync
games:x:5:60:games:/usr/games:/bin/sh
man:x:6:12:man:/var/cache/man:/bin/sh
lp:x:7:7:lp:/var/spool/lpd:/bin/sh
mail:x:8:8:mail:/var/mail:/bin/sh
news:x:9:9:news:/var/spool/news:/bin/sh
uucp:x:10:10:uucp:/var/spool/uucp:/bin/sh
proxy:x:13:13:proxy:/bin:/bin/sh
www-data:x:33:33:www-data:/var/www:/bin/sh
backup:x:34:34:backup:/var/backups:/bin/sh
list:x:38:38:Mailing List Manager:/var/list:/bin/sh
irc:x:39:39:ircd:/var/run/ircd:/bin/sh
gnats:x:41:41:Gnats Bug-Reporting System (admin):/var/lib/gnats:/bin/sh
nobody:x:65534:65534:nobody:/nonexistent:/bin/sh
Debian-exim:x:100:102::/var/spool/exim4:/bin/false
statd:x:101:65534::/var/lib/nfs:/bin/false
identd:x:102:65534::/var/run/identd:/bin/false
sshd:x:103:65534::/var/run/sshd:/usr/sbin/nologin
libuuid:x:104:104::/var/lib/libuuid:/bin/sh
xcapncrunchx:x:1000:1000:,,,:/home/xcapncrunchx:/bin/bash
ssh-agent:x:1001:1001:,,,:/home/ssh-agent:/bin/bash
ftp:x:105:65534::/home/ftp:/bin/false
mysql:x:106:106:MySQL Server,,,:/var/lib/mysql:/bin/false
postfix:x:107:107::/var/spool/postfix:/bin/false
dovecot:x:108:109:Dovecot mail server,,,:/usr/lib/dovecot:/bin/false
amavis:x:109:110:AMaViS system user,,,:/var/lib/amavis:/bin/sh
clamav:x:110:111::/var/lib/clamav:/bin/false
vmail:x:5050:5050::/var/vmail:/bin/sh
aestudio:x:1002:1002:,,,:/home/aestudio:/bin/bash
hereisthedeal:x:1003:1003:,,,:/home/hereisthedeal:/bin/bash
etribe:x:1004:1004:,,,:/home/etribe:/bin/bash
mycluster:x:1005:1005:,,,:/home/mycluster:/bin/bash
ntp:x:111:113::/home/ntp:/bin/false
uml-net:x:112:114::/home/uml-net:/bin/false


/* ---------------------
```

```
      /etc/resolv.conf
--------------------- */
nameserver 192.168.1.1
nameserver 8.8.8.8
nameserver 8.8.4.4
```

```
/* ------------------
      /etc/protcols
-------------------- */
```

Nota: Este archivo no se modifica durante el desarrollo de Linux Enterprise Sci-Fi.

```
/* ------------------
      /etc/services
-------------------- */
```

Nota: Este archivo no se modifica durante el desarrollo de Linux Enterprise Sci-Fi, pero se consultan los puertos asignados a procolos que contiene, especialmente el puerto 49 que en realidad corresponde al protocolo TACACS que se usa con SSH Secure Shell pero que luego se corrige también en los video programas para evitar confusiones entre servicios.

```
/* ---------------------------
      /etc/vsftpd.chroot_list
----------------------------- */
aestudio
xcapcrunchx
```

```
/* ---------------------
      /etc/vsftpd.conf
---------------------- */
#Example config file /etc/vsftpd.conf
#
# The default compiled in settings are fairly paranoid. This sample file
# loosens things up a bit, to make the ftp daemon more usable.
# Please see vsftpd.conf.5 for all compiled in defaults.
#
# READ THIS: This example file is NOT an exhaustive list of vsftpd
options.
# Please read the vsftpd.conf.5 manual page to get a full idea of vsftpd's
# capabilities.
#
#
```

```
# Run standalone? vsftpd can run either from an inetd or as a standalone
# daemon started from an initscript.
#listen=YES
listen=NO
#
# Run standalone with IPv6?
# Like the listen parameter, except vsftpd will listen on an IPv6 socket
# instead of an IPv4 one. This parameter and the listen parameter are
mutually
# exclusive.
#listen_ipv6=YES
#
# Allow anonymous FTP? (Beware - allowed by default if you comment
this out).
# <<< NEXT OPTION UPDATED! >>>
#anonymous_enable=YES
#
# Uncomment this to allow local users to log in.
# <<< NEXT OPTION UPDATED! >>>
local_enable=YES
#
# Uncomment this to enable any form of FTP write command.
write_enable=YES
#
# Default umask for local users is 077. You may wish to change this to 022,
# if your users expect that (022 is used by most other ftpd's)
# <<< NEXT OPTION UPDATED! >>>
local_umask=022
#
# Uncomment this to allow the anonymous FTP user to upload files. This
only
# has an effect if the above global write enable is activated. Also, you will
# obviously need to create a directory writable by the FTP user.
anon_upload_enable=YES
#
# Uncomment this if you want the anonymous FTP user to be able to
create
# new directories.
anon_mkdir_write_enable=YES
#
# Activate directory messages - messages given to remote users when they
# go into a certain directory.
# <<< NEXT OPTION UPDATED >>>
```

```
#dirmessage_enable=YES
#
# Activate logging of uploads/downloads.
xferlog_enable=YES
#
# Make sure PORT transfer connections originate from port 20 (ftp-data).
connect_from_port_20=YES
#
# If you want, you can arrange for uploaded anonymous files to be owned
by
# a different user. Note! Using "root" for uploaded files is not
# recommended!
#chown_uploads=YES
#chown_username=whoever
#
# You may override where the log file goes if you like. The default is shown
# below.
#xferlog_file=/var/log/vsftpd.log
#
# If you want, you can have your log file in standard ftpd xferlog format
#xferlog_std_format=YES
#
# You may change the default value for timing out an idle session.
# <<< NEXT OPTION UPDATED! >>>
idle_session_timeout=600
#
# You may change the default value for timing out a data connection.
# <<< NEXT OPTION UPDATED! >>>
data_connection_timeout=300
#
# It is recommended that you define on your system a unique user which
the
# ftp server can use as a totally isolated and unprivileged user.
#nopriv_user=ftpsecure
#
# Enable this and the server will recognise asynchronous ABOR requests.
Not
# recommended for security (the code is non-trivial). Not enabling it,
# however, may confuse older FTP clients.
# <<< NEXT LINE UPDATED! >>>
async_abor_enable=YES
#
# By default the server will pretend to allow ASCII mode but in fact ignore
```

the request. Turn on the below options to have the server actually do ASCII
mangling on files when in ASCII mode.
Beware that on some FTP servers, ASCII support allows a denial of service
attack (DoS) via the command "SIZE /big/file" in ASCII mode. vsftpd
predicted this attack and has always been safe, reporting the size of the
raw file.
ASCII mangling is a horrible feature of the protocol.
#ascii_upload_enable=YES
#ascii_download_enable=YES
#
# You may fully customise the login banner string:
# <<< NEXT LINE UPDATED! >>>
ftpd_banner=Welcome to aestudio.sytes.net FTP service.
#
You may specify a file of disallowed anonymous e-mail addresses. Apparently
useful for combatting certain DoS attacks.
#deny_email_enable=YES
(default follows)
#banned_email_file=/etc/vsftpd.banned_emails
#
# You may restrict local users to their home directories. See the FAQ for
# the possible risks in this before using chroot_local_user or
# chroot_list_enable below.
chroot_local_user=YES
#chroot_loca_users=YES
#chrott_local_users=YES

#
# You may specify an explicit list of local users to chroot() to their home
# directory. If chroot_local_user is YES, then this list becomes a list of
# users to NOT chroot().
# <<< NEXT LINE UPDATED! >>>
chroot_list_enable=YES
# (default follows)
# <<< NEXT LINE UPDATED >>>
chroot_list_file=/etc/vsftpd.chroot_list
#
You may activate the "-R" option to the builtin ls. This is disabled by
default to avoid remote users being able to cause excessive I/O on large
sites. However, some broken FTP clients such as "ncftp" and "mirror"

assume
the presence of the "-R" option, so there is a strong case for enabling it.
#ls_recurse_enable=YES
#
#
Debian customization
#
Some of vsftpd's settings don't fit the Debian filesystem layout by
default. These settings are more Debian-friendly.
#
# This option should be the name of a directory which is empty. Also, the
# directory should not be writable by the ftp user. This directory is used
# as a secure chroot() jail at times vsftpd does not require filesystem
# access.
secure_chroot_dir=/var/run/vsftpd
#
# This string is the name of the PAM service vsftpd will use.
pam_service_name=vsftpd
#
# This option specifies the location of the RSA certificate to use for SSL
# encrypted connections.
rsa_cert_file=/etc/ssl/certs/vsftpd.pem

# --== New added lines ==--
force_dot_files=NO
guest_enable=NO
hide_ids=YES
pasv_min_port=50000
pasv_max_port=60000
one_process_model=NO
accept_timeout=60
connect_timeout=300
max_per_ip=4
userlist_enable=YES
tcp_wrappers=YES
# The maximum data transfer rate permitted, in bytes per second,
# for local authenticated users:
#local_max_rate=10000

/* --------------------------
      /etc/vsftpd.user_list
-------------------------- */
      Nota: Este archivo se ha dejado en blanco.

```
/* --------------------
        /etc/xinetd.conf
---------------------- */
# Simple configuration file for xinetd
#
# Some defaults, and include /etc/xinetd.d/

defaults
{

# Please note that you need a log_type line to be able to use
log_on_success
# and log_on_failure. The default is the following :
# log_type = SYSLOG daemon info

}

includedir /etc/xinetd.d

/* ------------------------
        /etc/xinetd.d/csync2
-------------------------- */
service csync2
{
        disable         = no
        socket_type             = stream
        protocol        = tcp
        wait            = no
        user            = root
        server                  = /usr/sbin/csync2
        server_args             = -i
        log_type        = FILE /var/log/xinetd-csync2.log
        log_on_success          += HOST DURATION
        log_on_failure          += HOST
        instances       = 1
        cps             = 25 30
        port            = 30865
        type            = UNLISTED
        only_from               = x1.aestudio.sytes.net
        only_from               = 192.168.1.0/24
}
```

```
/* --------------------------------
      /etc/xinetd.d/dovecot-imap
-------------------------------- */
service imap
{
   disable       = no
   socket_type = stream
   protocol      = tcp
   wait          = no
   server        = /usr/lib/dovecot/imap-login
   user          = root
   log_type         = FILE /var/log/xinetd-imap.log
   log_on_success    += HOST DURATION
   log_on_failure    += HOST
   instances        = 60
   cps              = 25 30
}

/* --------------------------------
      /etc/xinetd.d/dovecot-pop3
-------------------------------- */
service pop3
{
   disable       = no
   socket_type = stream
   protocol      = tcp
   wait          = no
   server        = /usr/lib/dovecot/pop3-login
   user          = root
   log_type         = FILE /var/log/xinetd-pop3.log
   log_on_success    += HOST DURATION
   log_on_failure    += HOST
   instances        = 60
   cps              = 25 30
}

/* ------------------------
      /etc/xinetd.d/vsftp
------------------------ */
service ftp
{
      socket_type           = stream
      protocol              = tcp
```

```
wait              = no
user              = root
server            = /usr/sbin/vsftpd
log_type          = FILE /var/log/xinetd-ftp.log
log_on_success    += HOST DURATION
log_on_failure    += HOST
disable           = no
instances         = 60
cps               = 25 30
}


/* -------------------------------------------------------------------------
       /var/lib/vmware/Virtual    Machines/Virtual    Machine/Virtual
Machine.vmx
-------------------------------------------------------------------------- */
```

Nota: Este es un ejemplo del archivo de configurado de la máquina virtual que se autogenera al crear la máquina virtual en VMware® dentro del directorio de archivos de la máquina y se modifica al cambiar alguna de sus opciones, aunque es posible editarlo manualmente con mucho cuidado.

```
.encoding = "windows-1252"
config.version = "8"
virtualHW.version = "8"
memsize = "512"
MemAllowAutoScaleDown = "FALSE"
displayName = "Virtual Machine"
guestOS = "other"
numvcpus = "2"
usb.present = "TRUE"
vmci0.present = "TRUE"
ethernet0.present = "TRUE"
ethernet0.addressType = "generated"
ethernet0.connectionType = "bridged"
ethernet0.startConnected = "TRUE"
ide1:0.present = "TRUE"
ide1:0.autodetect = "TRUE"
ide1:0.filename = "auto detect"
ide1:0.deviceType = "cdrom-raw"
scsi0.present = "TRUE"
scsi0.virtualDev = "lsilogic"
scsi0:0.present = "TRUE"
scsi0:0.fileName = "Virtual Machine.vmdk"
lsilogic.noDriver = "FALSE"
ehci.present = "TRUE"
```

```
nvram = "Virtual Machine.nvram"
virtualHW.productCompatibility = "hosted"
ethernet0.features = "1"
vc.uuid = "52 3d 6e 39 9b 59 15 04-28 3f 7f e5 46 b0 4b a0"
scsi0:0.redo = ""
vmotion.checkpointFBSize = "33554432"
tools.remindInstall = "FALSE"
tools.syncTime = "false"
cleanShutdown = "TRUE"
replay.supported = "FALSE"
replay.filename = ""
usb.generic.allowHID = "TRUE"
snapshot.numRollingTiers = "3"
rollingTier0.uid = "1"
rollingTier0.interval = "86400"
rollingTier0.maximum = "1"
rollingTier0.clientFlags = "8"
rollingTier0.live = "TRUE"
rollingTier0.displayName = "AutoProtect Snapshot"
rollingTier1.uid = "2"
rollingTier1.interval = "604800"
rollingTier1.maximum = "1"
rollingTier1.baseTier = "1"
rollingTier1.baseTierInterval = "7"
rollingTier1.clientFlags = "8"
rollingTier1.live = "TRUE"
rollingTier1.displayName = "AutoProtect Snapshot"
rollingTier2.uid = "3"
rollingTier2.interval = "2419200"
rollingTier2.maximum = "1"
rollingTier2.baseTier = "1"
rollingTier2.baseTierInterval = "28"
rollingTier2.clientFlags = "8"
rollingTier2.live = "TRUE"
rollingTier2.displayName = "AutoProtect Snapshot"
rollingTier0.timeSincelast = "42586"
rollingTier1.timeSincelast = "40294"
rollingTier2.timeSincelast = "40294"
softPowerOff = "TRUE"
pciBridge0.present = "TRUE"
tools.upgrade.policy = "useGlobal"
pciBridge4.present = "TRUE"
pciBridge4.virtualDev = "pcieRootPort"
```

```
pciBridge5.present = "TRUE"
pciBridge5.virtualDev = "pcieRootPort"
pciBridge6.present = "TRUE"
pciBridge6.virtualDev = "pcieRootPort"
pciBridge7.present = "TRUE"
pciBridge7.virtualDev = "pcieRootPort"
extendedConfigFile = "Virtual Machine.vmxf"
scsi0.pciSlotNumber = "16"
ethernet0.generatedAddress = "00:0c:29:94:11:f1"
ethernet0.pciSlotNumber = "33"
usb.pciSlotNumber = "32"
ehci.pciSlotNumber = "34"
vmci0.id = "-711716367"
vmci0.pciSlotNumber = "35"
uuid.location = "56 4d eb 5a 2d 9c 74 36-03 1e cd 58 d5 94 11 f1"
uuid.bios = "56 4d eb 5a 2d 9c 74 36-03 1e cd 58 d5 94 11 f1"
pciBridge0.pciSlotNumber = "17"
pciBridge4.pciSlotNumber = "21"
pciBridge5.pciSlotNumber = "22"
pciBridge6.pciSlotNumber = "23"
pciBridge7.pciSlotNumber = "24"
usb:0.present = "TRUE"
usb:1.present = "TRUE"
ethernet0.generatedAddressOffset = "0"
usb:0.deviceType = "hid"
usb:0.port = "0"
usb:0.parent = "-1"
usb:1.speed = "2"
usb:1.deviceType = "hub"
usb:1.port = "1"
usb:1.parent = "-1"


/* ------------------------
    /etc/cron.d/awstats
-------------------------- */
*/10 * * * * www-data [ -x /usr/share/awstats/tools/update.sh ] &&
/usr/share/awstats/tools/update.sh

# Generate static reports:
10 03 * * * www-data [ -x /usr/share/awstats/tools/buildstatic.sh ] &&
/usr/share/awstats/tools/buildstatic.sh
```

En el espacio de root:

N/A

En el espacio de usuario:
```
/* ------------------------------------------------
     /home/aestudio/tmp/webalizer/webalizer.conf
----------------------------------------------- */
#
# Sample Webalizer configuration file
# Copyright 1997-2000 by Bradford L. Barrett (brad@mrunix.net)
#
# Distributed under the GNU General Public License.  See the
# files "Copyright" and "COPYING" provided with the webalizer
# distribution for additional information.
#
# This is a sample configuration file for the Webalizer (ver 2.01)
# Lines starting with pound signs '#' are comment lines and are
# ignored.  Blank lines are skipped as well.  Other lines are considered
# as configuration lines, and have the form "ConfigOption  Value" where
# ConfigOption is a valid configuration keyword, and Value is the value
# to assign that configuration option.  Invalid keyword/values are
# ignored, with appropriate warnings being displayed.  There must be
# at least one space or tab between the keyword and its value.
#
# As of version 0.98, The Webalizer will look for a 'default' configuration
# file named "webalizer.conf" in the current directory, and if not found
# there, will look for "/etc/webalizer.conf".


# LogFile defines the web server log file to use.  If not specified
# here or on on the command line, input will default to STDIN.  If
# the log filename ends in '.gz' (ie: a gzip compressed file), it will
# be decompressed on the fly as it is being read.

LogFile /var/log/apache2/aestudio.sytes.net.log

# LogType defines the log type being processed.  Normally, the Webalizer
# expects a CLF or Combined web server log as input.  Using this option,
# you can process ftp logs as well (xferlog as produced by wu-ftp and
# others), or Squid native logs.  Values can be 'clf', 'ftp' or 'squid',
# with 'clf' the default.

#LogType     clf
```

OutputDir is where you want to put the output files. This should
should be a full path name, however relative ones might work as well.
If no output directory is specified, the current directory will be used.

OutputDir /home/aestudio/tmp/webalizer

HistoryName allows you to specify the name of the history file produced
by the Webalizer. The history file keeps the data for up to 12 months
worth of logs, used for generating the main HTML page (index.html).
The default is a file named "webalizer.hist", stored in the specified
output directory. If you specify just the filename (without a path),
it will be kept in the specified output directory. Otherwise, the path
is relative to the output directory, unless absolute (leading /).

#HistoryName   webalizer.hist

Incremental processing allows multiple partial log files to be used
instead of one huge one. Useful for large sites that have to rotate
their log files more than once a month. The Webalizer will save its
internal state before exiting, and restore it the next time run, in
order to continue processing where it left off. This mode also causes
The Webalizer to scan for and ignore duplicate records (records already
processed by a previous run). See the README file for additional
information. The value may be 'yes' or 'no', with a default of 'no'.
The file 'webalizer.current' is used to store the current state data,
and is located in the output directory of the program (unless changed
with the IncrementalName option below). Please read at least the section
on Incremental processing in the README file before you enable this
option.

#Incremental no

IncrementalName allows you to specify the filename for saving the
incremental data in. It is similar to the HistoryName option where the
name is relative to the specified output directory, unless an absolute
filename is specified. The default is a file named "webalizer.current"
kept in the normal output directory. If you don't specify "Incremental"
as 'yes' then this option has no meaning.

#IncrementalName webalizer.current

ReportTitle is the text to display as the title. The hostname
(unless blank) is appended to the end of this string (seperated with

a space) to generate the final full title string.
Default is (for english) "Usage Statistics for".

ReportTitle Usage statistics for

HostName defines the hostname for the report. This is used in
the title, and is prepended to the URL table items. This allows
clicking on URL's in the report to go to the proper location in
the event you are running the report on a 'virtual' web server,
or for a server different than the one the report resides on.
If not specified here, or on the command line, webalizer will
try to get the hostname via a uname system call. If that fails,
it will default to "localhost".

HostName aestudio.sytes.net

HTMLExtension allows you to specify the filename extension to use
for generated HTML pages. Normally, this defaults to "html", but
can be changed for sites who need it (like for PHP embeded pages).

#HTMLExtension html

PageType lets you tell the Webalizer what types of URL's you
consider a 'page'. Most people consider html and cgi documents
as pages, while not images and audio files. If no types are
specified, defaults will be used ('htm*', 'cgi' and HTMLExtension
if different for web logs, 'txt' for ftp logs).

PageType htm*
PageType cgi
#PageType   phtml
PageType php3
#PageType   pl
PageType php

PagePrefix allows all requests with a specified prefix to be
considered as 'pages'. If you want everything under /documents
to be treated as pages no matter what their extension is. Also
useful if you have cgi-scripts with PATH_INFO.
#PagePrefix /mycgi/parameters

UseHTTPS should be used if the analysis is being run on a
secure server, and links to urls should use 'https://' instead

of the default 'http://'. If you need this, set it to 'yes'.
Default is 'no'. This only changes the behaviour of the 'Top
URL's' table.

#UseHTTPS   no

DNSCache specifies the DNS cache filename to use for reverse DNS
lookups.
This file must be specified if you wish to perform name lookups on any
IP
addresses found in the log file. If an absolute path is not given as
part of the filename (ie: starts with a leading '/'), then the name is
relative to the default output directory. See the DNS.README file for
additional information.

#DNSCache   dns_cache.db

DNSChildren allows you to specify how many "children" processes are
run to perform DNS lookups to create or update the DNS cache file.
If a number is specified, the DNS cache file will be created/updated
each time the Webalizer is run, immediately prior to normal processing,
by running the specified number of "children" processes to perform
DNS lookups. If used, the DNS cache filename MUST be specified as
well. The default value is zero (0), which disables DNS cache file
creation/updates at run time. The number of children processes to
run may be anywhere from 1 to 100, however a large number may effect
normal system operations. Reasonable values should be between 5 and
20. See the DNS.README file for additional information.

#DNSChildren   0

HTMLPre defines HTML code to insert at the very beginning of the
file. Default is the DOCTYPE line shown below. Max line length
is 80 characters, so use multiple HTMLPre lines if you need more.

#HTMLPre <!DOCTYPE HTML PUBLIC "-//W3C//DTD HTML 4.0
Transitional//EN">

HTMLHead   defines   HTML   code   to   insert   within   the
<HEAD></HEAD>
block, immediately after the <TITLE> line. Maximum line length
is 80 characters, so use multiple lines if needed.

#HTMLHead <META NAME="author" CONTENT="The Webalizer">

HTMLBody defined the HTML code to be inserted, starting with the
<BODY> tag. If not specified, the default is shown below. If
used, you MUST include your own <BODY> tag as the first line.
Maximum line length is 80 char, use multiple lines if needed.

#HTMLBody <BODY BGCOLOR="#E8E8E8" TEXT="#000000"
LINK="#0000FF" VLINK="#FF0000">

HTMLPost defines the HTML code to insert immediately before the
first <HR> on the document, which is just after the title and
"summary period"-"Generated on:" lines. If anything, this should
be used to clean up in case an image was inserted with HTMLBody.
As with HTMLHead, you can define as many of these as you want and
they will be inserted in the output stream in order of apperance.
Max string size is 80 characters. Use multiple lines if you need to.

#HTMLPost <BR CLEAR="all">

HTMLTail defines the HTML code to insert at the bottom of each
HTML document, usually to include a link back to your home
page or insert a small graphic. It is inserted as a table
data element (ie: <TD> your code here </TD>) and is right
alligned with the page. Max string size is 80 characters.

#HTMLTail <IMG SRC="msfree.png" ALT="100% Micro$oft free!">

HTMLEnd defines the HTML code to add at the very end of the
generated files. It defaults to what is shown below. If
used, you MUST specify the </BODY> and </HTML> closing tags
as the last lines. Max string length is 80 characters.

#HTMLEnd </BODY></HTML>

The Quiet option suppresses output messages... Useful when run
as a cron job to prevent bogus e-mails. Values can be either
"yes" or "no". Default is "no". Note: this does not suppress
warnings and errors (which are printed to stderr).

#Quiet   no

ReallyQuiet will supress all messages including errors and

warnings. Values can be 'yes' or 'no' with 'no' being the
default. If 'yes' is used here, it cannot be overriden from
the command line, so use with caution. A value of 'no' has
no effect.

#ReallyQuiet   no

TimeMe allows you to force the display of timing information
at the end of processing. A value of 'yes' will force the
timing information to be displayed. A value of 'no' has no
effect.

#TimeMe   no

GMTTime allows reports to show GMT (UTC) time instead of local
time. Default is to display the time the report was generated
in the timezone of the local machine, such as EDT or PST. This
keyword allows you to have times displayed in UTC instead. Use
only if you really have a good reason, since it will probably
screw up the reporting periods by however many hours your local
time zone is off of GMT.

#GMTTime   no

Debug prints additional information for error messages. This
will cause webalizer to dump bad records/fields instead of just
telling you it found a bad one. As usual, the value can be
either "yes" or "no". The default is "no". It shouldn't be
needed unless you start getting a lot of Warning or Error
messages and want to see why. (Note: warning and error messages
are printed to stderr, not stdout like normal messages).

#Debug   no

FoldSeqErr forces the Webalizer to ignore sequence errors.
This is useful for Netscape and other web servers that cache
the writing of log records and do not guarentee that they
will be in chronological order. The use of the FoldSeqErr
option will cause out of sequence log records to be treated
as if they had the same time stamp as the last valid record.
Default is to ignore out of sequence log records.

#FoldSeqErr no

VisitTimeout allows you to set the default timeout for a visit
(sometimes called a 'session'). The default is 30 minutes,
which should be fine for most sites.
Visits are determined by looking at the time of the current
request, and the time of the last request from the site. If
the time difference is greater than the VisitTimeout value, it
is considered a new visit, and visit totals are incremented.
Value is the number of seconds to timeout (default=1800=30min)

#VisitTimeout 1800

IgnoreHist shouldn't be used in a config file, but it is here
just because it might be usefull in certain situations. If the
history file is ignored, the main "index.html" file will only
report on the current log files contents. Usefull only when you
want to reproduce the reports from scratch. USE WITH CAUTION!
Valid values are "yes" or "no". Default is "no".

#IgnoreHist   no

Country Graph allows the usage by country graph to be disabled.
Values can be 'yes' or 'no', default is 'yes'.

#CountryGraph   yes

DailyGraph and DailyStats allows the daily statistics graph
and statistics table to be disabled (not displayed). Values
may be "yes" or "no". Default is "yes".

#DailyGraph   yes
#DailyStats   yes

HourlyGraph and HourlyStats allows the hourly statistics graph
and statistics table to be disabled (not displayed). Values
may be "yes" or "no". Default is "yes".

#HourlyGraph   yes
#HourlyStats yes

GraphLegend allows the color coded legends to be turned on or off
in the graphs. The default is for them to be displayed. This only
toggles the color coded legends, the other legends are not changed.

If you think they are hideous and ugly, say 'no' here :)

#GraphLegend   yes

GraphLines allows you to have index lines drawn behind the graphs.
I personally am not crazy about them, but a lot of people requested
them and they weren't a big deal to add. The number represents the
number of lines you want displayed. Default is 2, you can disable
the lines by using a value of zero ('0'). [max is 20]
Note, due to rounding errors, some values don't work quite right.
The lower the better, with 1,2,3,4,6 and 10 producing nice results.

#GraphLines 2

The "Top" options below define the number of entries for each table.
Defaults are Sites=30, URL's=30, Referrers=30 and Agents=15, and
Countries=30. TopKSites and TopKURLs (by KByte tables) both default
to 10, as do the top entry/exit tables (TopEntry/TopExit). The top
search strings and usernames default to 20. Tables may be disabled
by using zero (0) for the value.

#TopSites   30
#TopKSites   10
#TopURLs   30
#TopKURLs   10
#TopReferrers 30
#TopAgents   15
#TopCountries 30
#TopEntry   10
#TopExit   10
#TopSearch   20
#TopUsers   20

The All* keywords allow the display of all URL's, Sites, Referrers
User Agents, Search Strings and Usernames. If enabled, a seperate
HTML page will be created, and a link will be added to the bottom
of the appropriate "Top" table. There are a couple of conditions
for this to occur.. First, there must be more items than will fit
in the "Top" table (otherwise it would just be duplicating what is
already displayed). Second, the listing will only show those items
that are normally visable, which means it will not show any hidden
items. Grouped entries will be listed first, followed by individual
items. The value for these keywords can be either 'yes' or 'no',

with the default being 'no'. Please be aware that these pages can
be quite large in size, particularly the sites page, and seperate
pages are generated for each month, which can consume quite a lot
of disk space depending on the traffic to your site.

#AllSites no
#AllURLs   no
#AllReferrers no
#AllAgents   no
#AllSearchStr no
#AllUsers   no

The Webalizer normally strips the string 'index.' off the end of
URL's in order to consolidate URL totals. For example, the URL
/somedir/index.html is turned into /somedir/ which is really the
same URL. This option allows you to specify additional strings
to treat in the same way. You don't need to specify 'index.' as
it is always scanned for by The Webalizer, this option is just to
specify _additional_ strings if needed. If you don't need any,
don't specify any as each string will be scanned for in EVERY
log record... A bunch of them will degrade performance. Also,
the string is scanned for anywhere in the URL, so a string of
'home' would turn the URL /somedir/homepages/brad/home.html into
just /somedir/ which is probably not what was intended.

#IndexAlias   home.htm
#IndexAlias   homepage.htm

The Hide*, Group* and Ignore* and Include* keywords allow you to
change the way Sites, URL's, Referrers, User Agents and Usernames
are manipulated. The Ignore* keywords will cause The Webalizer to
completely ignore records as if they didn't exist (and thus not
counted in the main site totals). The Hide* keywords will prevent
things from being displayed in the 'Top' tables, but will still be
counted in the main totals. The Group* keywords allow grouping
similar objects as if they were one. Grouped records are displayed
in the 'Top' tables and can optionally be displayed in BOLD and/or
shaded. Groups cannot be hidden, and are not counted in the main
totals. The Group* options do not, by default, hide all the items
that it matches. If you want to hide the records that match (so just
the grouping record is displayed), follow with an identical Hide*
keyword with the same value. (see example below) In addition,
Group* keywords may have an optional label which will be displayed

```
# instead of the keywords value.  The label should be seperated from
# the value by at least one 'white-space' character, such as a space
# or tab.
#
# The value can have either a leading or trailing '*' wildcard
# character.  If no wildcard is found, a match can occur anywhere
# in the string. Given a string "www.yourmama.com", the values "your",
# "*mama.com" and "www.your*" will all match.

# Your own site should be hidden
#HideSite       *mrunix.net
#HideSite       localhost

# Your own site gives most referrals
#HideReferrer mrunix.net/

# This one hides non-referrers ("-" Direct requests)
#HideReferrer Direct Request

# Usually you want to hide these
HideURL        *.gif
HideURL        *.GIF
HideURL        *.jpg
HideURL        *.JPG
HideURL        *.png
HideURL        *.PNG
HideURL        *.ra

# Hiding agents is kind of futile
#HideAgent     RealPlayer

# You can also hide based on authenticated username
#HideUser      root
#HideUser      admin

# Grouping options
#GroupURL  /cgi-bin/*      CGI Scripts
#GroupURL  /images/*       Images

#GroupSite    *.aol.com
#GroupSite    *.compuserve.com

#GroupReferrer    yahoo.com/    Yahoo!
```

```
#GroupReferrer    excite.com/    Excite
#GroupReferrer    infoseek.com/   InfoSeek
#GroupReferrer    webcrawler.com/ WebCrawler

#GroupUser    root        Admin users
#GroupUser    admin       Admin users
#GroupUser    wheel       Admin users
```

The following is a great way to get an overall total
for browsers, and not display all the detail records.
(You should use MangleAgent to refine further...)

```
#GroupAgent MSIE          Micro$oft Internet Exploder
#HideAgent   MSIE
#GroupAgent Mozilla       Netscape
#HideAgent   Mozilla
#GroupAgent Lynx*         Lynx
#HideAgent   Lynx*
```

HideAllSites allows forcing individual sites to be hidden in the
report. This is particularly useful when used in conjunction
with the "GroupDomain" feature, but could be useful in other
situations as well, such as when you only want to display grouped
sites (with the GroupSite keywords...). The value for this
keyword can be either 'yes' or 'no', with 'no' the default,
allowing individual sites to be displayed.

#HideAllSites no

The GroupDomains keyword allows you to group individual hostnames
into their respective domains. The value specifies the level of
grouping to perform, and can be thought of as 'the number of dots'
that will be displayed. For example, if a visiting host is named
cust1.tnt.mia.uu.net, a domain grouping of 1 will result in just
"uu.net" being displayed, while a 2 will result in "mia.uu.net".
The default value of zero disable this feature. Domains will only
be grouped if they do not match any existing "GroupSite" records,
which allows overriding this feature with your own if desired.

#GroupDomains   0

The GroupShading allows grouped rows to be shaded in the report.
Useful if you have lots of groups and individual records that

```
# intermingle in the report, and you want to diferentiate the group
# records a little more.  Value can be 'yes' or 'no', with 'yes'
# being the default.

#GroupShading     yes

# GroupHighlight allows the group record to be displayed in BOLD.
# Can be either 'yes' or 'no' with the default 'yes'.

#GroupHighlight   yes

# The Ignore* keywords allow you to completely ignore log records based
# on hostname, URL, user agent, referrer or username.  I hessitated in
# adding these, since the Webalizer was designed to generate _accurate_
# statistics about a web servers performance.  By choosing to ignore
# records, the accuracy of reports become skewed, negating why I wrote
# this program in the first place.  However, due to popular demand, here
# they are.  Use the same as the Hide* keywords, where the value can have
# a leading or trailing wildcard '*'.  Use at your own risk ;)

#IgnoreSite     bad.site.net
IgnoreSite      localhost
#IgnoreURL  /test*
#IgnoreReferrer    file:/*
IgnoreReferrer localhost
#IgnoreAgent RealPlayer
#IgnoreUser     root

# The Include* keywords allow you to force the inclusion of log records
# based on hostname, URL, user agent, referrer or username.  They take
# precidence over the Ignore* keywords.  Note: Using Ignore/Include
# combinations to selectivly process parts of a web site is _extremely
# inefficent_!!! Avoid doing so if possible (ie: grep the records to a
# seperate file if you really want that kind of report).

# Example: Only show stats on Joe User's pages...
#IgnoreURL  *
#IncludeURL ~joeuser*

# Or based on an authenticated username
#IgnoreUser     *
#IncludeUser    someuser
```

The MangleAgents allows you to specify how much, if any, The Webalizer
should mangle user agent names. This allows several levels of detail
to be produced when reporting user agent statistics. There are six
levels that can be specified, which define different levels of detail
supression. Level 5 shows only the browser name (MSIE or Mozilla)
and the major version number. Level 4 adds the minor version number
(single decimal place). Level 3 displays the minor version to two
decimal places. Level 2 will add any sub-level designation (such
as Mozilla/3.01Gold or MSIE 3.0b). Level 1 will attempt to also add
the system type if it is specified. The default Level 0 displays the
full user agent field without modification and produces the greatest
amount of detail. User agent names that can't be mangled will be
left unmodified.

#MangleAgents   0

The SearchEngine keywords allow specification of search engines and
their query strings on the URL. These are used to locate and report
what search strings are used to find your site. The first word is
a substring to match in the referrer field that identifies the search
engine, and the second is the URL variable used by that search engine
to define it's search terms.

SearchEngine yahoo.com   p=
SearchEngine altavista.com   q=
SearchEngine google.com   q=
SearchEngine eureka.com   q=
SearchEngine lycos.com query=
SearchEngine hotbot.com   MT=
SearchEngine msn.com   MT=
SearchEngine infoseek.com   qt=
SearchEngine webcrawler   searchText=
SearchEngine excite   search=
SearchEngine netscape.com   search=
SearchEngine mamma.com   query=
SearchEngine alltheweb.com query=
SearchEngine northernlight.com qr=
SearchEngine sensis.com.au   find=
SearchEngine google.nl q=
SearchEngine google.fr q=
SearchEngine google.ch q=
SearchEngine google.ca q=

SearchEngine google.be q=

The Dump* keywords allow the dumping of Sites, URL's, Referrers
User Agents, Usernames and Search strings to seperate tab delimited
text files, suitable for import into most database or spreadsheet
programs.

DumpPath specifies the path to dump the files. If not specified,
it will default to the current output directory. Do not use a
trailing slash ('/').

#DumpPath   /var/lib/httpd/logs

The DumpHeader keyword specifies if a header record should be
written to the file. A header record is the first record of the
file, and contains the labels for each field written. Normally,
files that are intended to be imported into a database system
will not need a header record, while spreadsheets usually do.
Value can be either 'yes' or 'no', with 'no' being the default.

#DumpHeader   no

DumpExtension allow you to specify the dump filename extension
to use. The default is "tab", but some programs are pickey about
the filenames they use, so you may change it here (for example,
some people may prefer to use "csv").

#DumpExtension tab

These control the dumping of each individual table. The value
can be either 'yes' or 'no'.. the default is 'no'.

#DumpSites   no
#DumpURLs no
#DumpReferrers   no
#DumpAgents   no
#DumpUsers no
#DumpSearchStr no

If you compiled Webalizer with GeoIP library, it becomes enabled
by default. But if you wish to disable it, just set GeoIP to 'no'.
You may also want to specify database file path manually, if you
don't have one installed on system (in case of static build).

```
GeoIP          yes
GeoIPDatabase    /usr/share/GeoIP/GeoIP.dat

# The custom  bar graph Colors are defined here. Declare them
# in the standard hexadecimal way (as HTML, without the '#')
# If none are given, you will get the standard webalizer colors.


#ColorHit     00805c
#ColorFile    0000ff
#ColorSite    ff8000
#ColorKbyte   ff0000
#ColorPage    00c0ff
#ColorVisit   ffff00


#PieColor1    800080
#PieColor2    80ffc0
#PieColor3    ff00ff
#PieColor4    ffc480


# TrueTypeFont makes possible to replace GD built-in font by
# specified TrueTypeFont.
# The value can be '/path/to/your/true_type_font.file' or empty.
# If value is empty(or commented out), GD built-in font will be used.
# The default is empty.
# (Supplement for Japanese:
#  Under EUC-JP locale, TTF file must be specified which has *Windows
#  Shift-JIS encoding*. This limitation is derived from libgd.
#  e.g. you can use "/usr/share/fonts/truetype/X-TT/wadalab-gothic.ttf"
#  provided by ttf-xtt-wadalab-gothic package)


#TrueTypeFont

# End of configuration file...  Have a nice day!


/* ------------------------------------
    /home/mycluster/conf/config.ini
------------------------------------- */
```

Nota: Este archivo es una configuración básica de MySQL Cluster 7.2. Queda pendiente agregarle la línea para especificar el directorio, partición o disco de BACKUP de las bases de datos, a como se explica en los DVDs de Cluster de Linux Enterprise Sci Fi. Se puede consultar también la documentación oficial de Oracle® MySQL Cluster. (Ver archivo de

configurado de mysql cluster versión 5.0).
[ndb_mgmd]
hostname=localhost
datadir=/home/mycluster/ndb_data
NodeId=1

[ndbd default]
noofreplicas=2
DataMemory=256M
IndexMemory=64M
datadir=/home/mycluster/ndb_data

[ndbd]
hostname=localhost

NodeId=3

[ndbd]
hostname=localhost

NodeId=4

[mysqld]
NodeId=50

```
/* --------------------------------
      /home/mycluster/conf/my.ini
-------------------------------- */
```
[mysqld]
ndbcluster
datadir=/home/mycluster/mysqld_data
basedir=/home/mycluster/mysqlc
port=5000

```
/* ----------------------------
      /home/xcapncrunchx/.ssh/
------------------------------ */
```

En este directorio deben existir los archivos: authorized_keys, known_hosts, x2..1 y x1..x2

No se han adjuntado ningún otro de los archivos llave (keys) generados automáticamente como llaves públicas o privadas o certificados SSL de ningún tipo.

3 SCRIPTS EJECUTABLES

Todos los scripts de la presente sección funcionan correctamente, pero aunque nunca me ha pasado, su ejecución podría llegar a fallar en determinado momento, por lo que recomiendo antes del exit final en cada uno de ellos agregar alguna líaea como:
echo "Se ejecutó?:" $?

El programa retornará a shell el contenido de la variable de ambiente $?, que debe ser 0 ó 1. 0 generalmente quiere decir que el programa se completó y 1 que ha fallado. Es posible agregar más código con bucles para repetir la ejecución de un script completo en caso de fallo y mostrar un mensaje en la consola, leyendo el contenido de esta variable, de ser necesario. También puede optar por terminar los scripts con un simple exit 0.

Host: foobar.
Función: Servidor de virtualización VMware®, KVM o similares. Load balancer y proxy.
Scripts ejecutables:

```
/* -------------------------------------------------
        /home/xcapncrunchx/Compress-kvm-system-isos.sh
-------------------------------------------------- */
# Compress kvm hosts images:
# (Adapt to your requirements)
tar        -cvzpf        /hd2/x1.tgz        2>/hd2/error-x1.log
/var/lib/libvirt/images/x1.qcow2
tar        -cvzpf        /hd2/x1-config.tgz        2>/hd2/error-x1-config.log
/var/lib/libvirt/qemu/x1.xml
tar        -cvzpf        /hd2/x2.tgz        2>/hd2/error-x2.log
/var/lib/libvirt/images/x2.qcow2
```

```
tar      -cvzpf      /hd2/x2-config.tgz      2>/hd2/error-x2-config.log
/var/lib/libvirt/qemu/x2.xml
# And then give a name to the servers backups:
# X1-001-03-29-14-AFTER-HOSTNAME+FQDN.tgz
# X1-001-03-29-14-AFTER-HOSTNAME+FQDN-SETUP.tgz
# X2-001-03-29-14-AFTER-HOSTNAME+FQDN.tgz
# X2-001-03-29-14-AFTER-HOSTNAME+FQDN-SETUP.tgz
exit


/* --------------------------------------------------
      /home/xcapncrunchx/Extract-kvm-system-isos.sh
-------------------------------------------------- */
# Extract virtual Machines:
# (Adapt to your requirements)
cd /
cp          -dpR          /hd2/servers-x1/X1-001-03-29-14-AFTER-
HOSTNAME+FQDN.tgz ./
cp          -dpR          /hd2/servers-x1/X1-001-03-29-14-AFTER-
HOSTNAME+FQDN-SETUP.tgz ./
cp          -dpR          /hd2/servers-x1/X2-001-03-29-14-AFTER-
HOSTNAME+FQDN.tgz ./
cp          -dpR          /hd2/servers-x1/X2-001-03-29-14-AFTER-
HOSTNAME+FQDN-SETUP.tgz ./
tar xvzf X1-001-03-29-14-AFTER-HOSTNAME+FQDN.tgz
tar xvzf X1-001-03-29-14-AFTER-HOSTNAME+FQDN-SETUP.tgz
tar xvzf X2-001-03-29-14-AFTER-HOSTNAME+FQDN.tgz
tar xvzf X2-001-03-29-14-AFTER-HOSTNAME+FQDN-SETUP.tgz
exit


/* -------------------------------------
      /home/xcapncrunchx/backuptouch.sh
------------------------------------- */
#!/bin/sh
# Name: backuptouch.sh
# Execution: Automatically, every day, at 3 a.m.
# or before system changes.
# Machine: server, backup-server
# Allocation: /home/esteban/
#
# Forces the filesystems (partitions) check at startup:
touch /forcefsck
# Reboot the machine
reboot
```

exit
#

/* ---------------------------------
    /home/xcapncrunchx/backup.sh
--------------------------------- */
#!/bin/sh
Name: backup.sh
Execution: Automatically, every day, at 3:30 a.m,
or Manually, whenever you need, after or before special (good,bad) events.
Machine: server, backup-server
Allocation: /home/esteban/
(Adjust to your needs)
#
Summary of some important directories:
/home > user files, web files (for our installation, can be other like /var), etc. remember some.
programs have users, like FTP.
/var > databases, apache logs, etc.
/usr > where "source" programs are installed, some program require creation of files and directories.
/etc > configuration's files.
/tmp > for post-morten analysis.
/bin > executables of programs.
Some system files:
/dev > Do not include in the backup, the files of devices like hard discs, etc.
/swap > Do not include in the backup, but can be necessary for post-morten analysis.
/sys > Do not include in the backup, the restoration will not work.
/proc > Do not include in the backup, the restoration will not work.
#
When the backup is run manually during the day or at "working hours", consider while
the system is being rebooted, the client's services will not work.
#
Creates the package, compress and paste the system dirs the second hard disc:
Some dirs are partitions, others are directories under /. We are using
partitions for dirs /tmp, /usr, /var, /home.
cd /hd2
Instead of 'cd' we would probably use the flag -C at the tar command's

end followed by the path
to the file, to define the path to it there. Every option begins with two of
"-", eg. - - exclude...:
tar -cvzpf /hd2/dirs.tgz –same-owner –exclude=/initrd/* --
exclude=/hd2/* --exclude=/home/error.log --exclude=/proc/* --
exclude=/media/* --exclude=/dev/* --exclude=/mnt/* --exclude=/sys/*
--exclude=/tmp/* / 2>/home/error.log
tgz is the same to say .tar.gz, but MS windows readable extensions.
Sends a copy of the backup to the backup-server:
Edit your -p=PORT as ssh is listening
The user before @ is the same user, configured in the server and the
backup-server.
Substitute the part of the line IP-or-FQDN by the server backup IP
address.
Next line is incomplete, to complete it if you need to sync see rsync
scripts and modify it accordingly. If you don't do it the program only is
going backup and will skip teh synchronization.
rsync -vv -e "ssh -p 49" /hd2/dirs.tar.gz esteban@IP-
orFQDN:/home/esteban
To create "milestones" (system restoration points or states) rename the
backups before
the backup is executed again. E.G.: 6660001-03-05-2010-8.2-dirs.tar.gz
#
After the back is made run this to verify the new dirs.tar.gz file's integrity
(in the server and in the backup server):
sh> tar -tvzf /hd2/dirs.tgz 2>/home/error2.log
exit

/* --------------------------------------
        /home/xcapncrunchx/restoration.sh
-------------------------------------- */
#!/bin/sh
Name: restoration.sh
(Adjust to your requirements)
Execution: When system is destroyed after a new system installation or
formatted,
to be executed since the a Live distro DVD like Knoppix or floppy disc.
or when we need to roll back changes on files.
Machine: server, backup-server
Allocation: /hd2
#
To know exactly what directories are in the backup, read the script file
backup.sh.

```
#
# Remember while the system is under restoration will not work, consider
the clients and their
# processes.
#
# Create the filesystem's root in the second hd hd2 due to there the change
is permanent
# and there is more space than in RAM or /swap:
mkdir /mnt/hd2/gentoo
# Mount the partitions you created during the system's installation or you
have in your system
# to retore. Remember some like /swap /proc and /sys were not included
during the
# backup process because the restoration process will not work. See the
backup file
# backup.sh
cd /mnt/hd2
cd ..
# mount the HD1 in HD2 to be accessed from the Live System:
# Note the / directory is not in the backup but is mounted. Things that
aren't partitions were
# not included as devices, they haven't them, but are under /, e.g. the dir
/bin, etc.
# Changes can be made here depending on our needs and devices use our
system.
mount /dev/hda1 /mnt/hd2/gentoo/
mount /dev/hda5 /mnt/hd2/gentoo/usr
mount /dev/hda6 /mnt/hd2/gentoo/var
mount /dev/hda8 /mnt/hd2/gentoo/tmp
mount /dev/hda9 /mnt/hd2/gentoo/home
# Paste the backup file dirs.tar.gz (or the renamed milestone) on the HD1
crashed mounted system,
# restoring it:
cd /mnt/hd2/gentoo
# Instead of 'cd' we would probably use the flag -C at the tar command's
end followed by  the path
# to the file, to define the path to it there where the files will be extracted.
tar -xvzpf /mnt/hd2/dirs.tgz
# Once the de-compress process finish, umount the filesystem to a avoid
destroy their information:
# I will do it ten times un til the system's cron to unmount responds ;-)))
cd /
umount /dev/hda*
```

```
umount /dev/hda*
umount /dev/hda*
umount /dev/hda*
umount /dev/hda*
umount /dev/hda*
umount /dev/hda*
umount /dev/hda*
umount /dev/hda*
umount /dev/hda*
# Know the refreshed system is restored and prepared.
# Umount the second hard disk:
umount /dev/hdb1
umount /dev/hdb1
umount /dev/hdb1
umount /dev/hdb1
umount /dev/hdb1
umount /dev/hdb1
umount /dev/hdb1
umount /dev/hdb1
umount /dev/hdb1
#
exit


/* -----------------------------
    /home/xcapncrunchx/pen.sh
----------------------------- */
!#/bin/sh
### BEGIN INIT INFO
# Provides:        pen
# Required-Start:  $local_fs $network
# Required-Stop:   $local_fs
# Default-Start:   2 3 4 5
# Default-Stop:    0 1 6
# Short-Description: pen
# Description:      pen load balancer and proxy daemon
### END INIT INFO
# Distribuites the workload between the servers in the cluster.
# -------------------------------------------------------------
# To Re-configure Pen in real time on the fly:
# A- Kill previous running Pen:
#ps -aux | grep pen
#kill <PID>
```

```
# B- Add a new Proxy rule:
#pen -r -a -d Load-balancer-IP:PORT> <cluster-host-1-IP:PORT>
<cluster-host-n-IP:PORT> ...
# You can redirect from one port number in the loadbalancer to a another
port number
# in the cluster ( high availability )host.
# C- To limit the max amount of connections:
# Here three servers cooperate in a web server farm. Host www1 runs its
web server on
# port 8000 and accepts a maximum of 10 simultaneous connections.
Host www2
# runs on port 80 and accepts 10 connections. Finally, www3 runs its web
server on port
# 80 and allows an unlimited number of simultaneous connections.
#pen 80 www1:8000:10 www2:80:10 www3
# D- To block all the connections by running a new pen command in
mode FOREFRONT:
#pen -r -a -d -f Load-balancer-IP:PORT> <cluster-host-1-IP:PORT>
<cluster-host-n-IP:PORT> ...
# ------------------------------------------------------------
# System boot up rules:
# Update any changes on firewall scripts in the route like include
# bastion-server-firewall.sh
# Don't include port 22 which is for ssh because PEN will don't forward it.
# Anyway we need this ports not forwarded to access the load balancer
# through secure shell.
# Ports list:
# ntp:            123
# MySQL Cluster:       1186
# ftp:           21
# http (web):       80
# https (web):      443
# imap:           143
# imap3:          220
# imaps:          993
# pop2:           109
# pop3:           110
# pop3s:          995
# smtp:           25
# ssmtp:          465
# ...
pen -r -a 192.168.1.199:123 192.168.1.200:123 192.168.1.205:123
pen -r -a 192.168.1.199:1186 192.168.1.200:1186 192.168.1.205:1186
```

```
pen -r -a 192.168.1.199:21 192.168.1.200:21 192.168.1.205:21
pen -r -a 192.168.1.199:80 192.168.1.200:80 192.168.1.205:80
pen -r -a 192.168.1.199:443 192.168.1.200:443 192.168.1.205:443
pen -r -a 192.168.1.199:143 192.168.1.200:143 192.168.1.205:143
pen -r -a 192.168.1.199:220 192.168.1.200:220 192.168.1.205:220
pen -r -a 192.168.1.199:993 192.168.1.200:993 192.168.1.205:993
pen -r -a 192.168.1.199:109 192.168.1.200:109 192.168.1.205:109
pen -r -a 192.168.1.199:110 192.168.1.200:110 192.168.1.205:110
pen -r -a 192.168.1.199:995 192.168.1.200:995 192.168.1.205:995
pen -r -a 192.168.1.199:25 192.168.1.200:25 192.168.1.205:25
pen -r -a 192.168.1.199:465 192.168.1.200:465 192.168.1.205:465
#
#
# Once the balancers are up and running it's time to bind the virtual ip
# on the balancer's IP:
#sh /etc/init.d/pen-virtual-ip.sh

exit

/* ----------------------------------------
      /home/xcapncrunchx/pen-virtual-ip.sh
---------------------------------------- */
!#/bin/sh
### BEGIN INIT INFO
# Provides:         Virtual IP vrrpd
# Required-Start:   $local_fs $network
# Required-Stop:    $local_fs
# Default-Start:    2 3 4 5
# Default-Stop:     0 1 6
# Short-Description: Virtual IP vrrpd
# Description:      Virtual IP vrrpd script
### END INIT INFO
# Bind host ip addresses set in eth0 to create virtual IP address
(192.168.1.197)
# Now try surfing to http://192.168.1.197/. One of the load balancers will
be active
# and respond at that address. Disconnect that load balancer from the
network to
# simulate a failure. Now the other load balancer will take over the address,
# restoring functionality.
# In the example network, the firewall uses NAT, although that is in no
way
# necessary. A Cisco PIX would be configured something like this:
```

static (inside,outside) 193.12.6.25 10.1.1.4 netmask 255.255.255.255 0 0
conduit permit tcp host 193.12.6.25 eq 80 any
vrrpd -i eth0 -v 1 192.168.1.197

exit

El script correspondiente al parche de VMware® Server aplicado a las versiones del host foobar con Debian Squeeze no se encuentra en este libro. De todos modos no se recomienda utilizar VMware® Server ya que ha sido descontinuado (Ver Archivos de configurado VMware® y Virtualizacion KVM en este libro y en los DVDs LE SF. En el DVD LE SF 2 se encuentran todos los pasos para modificar el script y aplicar el parche para Debian GNU/Linux Squeeze si aún desea continuar usando VMware® versión Server).

Host: x2.
Función: Servidor en granja de servidores o cluster HA de máxima disponibilidad basado en el servidor bastión stand-alone aestudio con todos los servicios disponibles.
Scripts ejecutables:
```
* ----------------------------------------
      /home/aetudio/public_html/index.html
----------------------------------------- */
<html>
    <title> Test </title>
    Welcome to http://aestudio.sytes.net/
</html>


* ----------------------------------------
      Email server MySQL database tables
----------------------------------------- */
```
Nota: Esta sección no es un archivo, sino que contiene los comandos para consola de PHPMyAdmin o línea de comandos, aunque se puede modificar para agregarse dentro de algún otro archivo como crear-db.php, mysqlworkbench-db.sql o equivalente.
Create the database tables:
```
mysql> CREATE TABLE `virtual_domains` (
    id INT(11) NOT NULL auto_increment,
    name VARCHAR(50) NOT NULL,
    PRIMARY KEY (id)
    ) ENGINE = InnoDB;
mysql> CREATE TABLE `virtual_users` (
    id int(11) NOT NULL auto_increment,
```

```
        domain_id INT(11) NOT NULL,
        user VARCHAR(40) NOT NULL,
        password VARCHAR(32) NOT NULL,
        CONSTRAINT UNIQUE_EMAIL UNIQUE (domain_id,user),
        FOREIGN KEY (domain_id) REFERENCES virtual_domains(id)
ON      DELETE CASCADE,
        PRIMARY KEY (id)
) ENGINE = InnoDB;
mysql> CREATE TABLE `virtual_aliases` (
        id int(11) NOT NULL auto_increment,
        domain_id INT(11) NOT NULL,
        source VARCHAR(40) NOT NULL,
        destination VARCHAR(80) NOT NULL,
        FOREIGN KEY (domain_id) REFERENCES virtual_domains(id)
ON      DELETE CASCADE,
        PRIMARY KEY (id)
) ENGINE = InnoDB;
```

Alter table to add email space quotas:
```
mysql> ALTER TABLE `virtual_users` ADD `quota_kb` INT NOT NULL,
ADD `quota_messages` INT NOT NULL ;
```

Create users view:
```
mysql> CREATE VIEW view_users AS
        SELECT CONCAT(virtual_users.user, '@', virtual_domains.name) AS email,
        virtual_users.password,                virtual_users.quota_kb,
virtual_users.quota_messages
        FROM virtual_users
        LEFT            JOIN    virtual_domains                 ON
virtual_users.domain_id=virtual_domains.id;
```

```
* -------------------------------------------
        TOTAL-EMAIL-DOMAINS-USERS-ALIASES.SQL
-------------------------------------------- */
INSERT INTO virtual_domains (id, name) VALUES (1, 'aestudio.sytes.net');
INSERT INTO virtual_domains (id, name) VALUES (2, 'aestudio000.zapto.org');
INSERT INTO virtual_domains (id, name) VALUES (3, 'etribe.sytes.net');
INSERT INTO virtual_domains (id, name) VALUES (4, 'hereisthedeal.hopto.org');
```

INSERT INTO virtual_domains (id, name) VALUES (5, 'localhost');

INSERT INTO virtual_users (id, domain_id, user, password, quota_kb, quota_messages)
    VALUES (1, 5, 'root', MD5('PASSWORD_HERE'), 1000000, 1000000);
INSERT INTO virtual_users (id, domain_id, user, password, quota_kb, quota_messages)
    VALUES (2, 1, 'root', MD5('PASSWORD_HERE'), 1000000, 1000000);
INSERT INTO virtual_users (id, domain_id, user, password, quota_kb, quota_messages)
    VALUES (3, 1, 'postmaster', MD5('PASSWORD_HERE'), 1000000, 1000000);
INSERT INTO virtual_users (id, domain_id, user, password, quota_kb, quota_messages)
    VALUES (4, 1, 'xcapncrunchx', MD5('PASSWORD_HERE'), 1000000, 1000000);
INSERT INTO virtual_users (id, domain_id, user, password, quota_kb, quota_messages)
    VALUES (5, 1, 'webmaster', MD5('PASSWORD_HERE'), 1000000, 1000000);
INSERT INTO virtual_users (id, domain_id, user, password, quota_kb, quota_messages)
    VALUES (6, 1, 'aestudio', MD5('PASSWORD_HERE'), 1000000, 1000000);
INSERT INTO virtual_users (id, domain_id, user, password, quota_kb, quota_messages)
    VALUES (7, 1, 'lev', MD5('PASSWORD_HERE'), 1000000, 1000000);
INSERT INTO virtual_users (id, domain_id, user, password, quota_kb, quota_messages)
    VALUES (8, 1, 'myname', MD5('PASSWORD_HERE'), 1000000, 1000000);
INSERT INTO virtual_users (id, domain_id, user, password, quota_kb, quota_messages)
    VALUES (9, 1, 'contact', MD5('PASSWORD_HERE'), 1000000, 1000000);
INSERT INTO virtual_users (id, domain_id, user, password, quota_kb, quota_messages)
    VALUES (10, 1, 'noreply', MD5('PASSWORD_HERE'), 1000000, 1000000);

```
INSERT INTO virtual_users (id, domain_id, user, password, quota_kb,
quota_messages)
        VALUES (11, 4, 'webmaster', MD5('PASSWORD_HERE'),
1000000, 1000000);
INSERT INTO virtual_users (id, domain_id, user, password, quota_kb,
quota_messages)
        VALUES (12, 4, 'hereisthedeal', MD5('PASSWORD_HERE'),
1000000, 1000000);
INSERT INTO virtual_users (id, domain_id, user, password, quota_kb,
quota_messages)
        VALUES (13, 4, 'myname', MD5('PASSWORD_HERE'), 1000000,
1000000);
INSERT INTO virtual_users (id, domain_id, user, password, quota_kb,
quota_messages)
        VALUES (14, 4, 'contact', MD5('PASSWORD_HERE'), 1000000,
1000000);
INSERT INTO virtual_users (id, domain_id, user, password, quota_kb,
quota_messages)
        VALUES (15, 4, 'noreply', MD5('PASSWORD_HERE'), 1000000,
1000000);

INSERT INTO virtual_users (id, domain_id, user, password, quota_kb,
quota_messages)
        VALUES (16, 3, 'webmaster', MD5('PASSWORD_HERE'),
1000000, 1000000);
INSERT INTO virtual_users (id, domain_id, user, password, quota_kb,
quota_messages)
        VALUES (17, 3, 'etribe', MD5('PASSWORD_HERE'), 1000000,
1000000);
INSERT INTO virtual_users (id, domain_id, user, password, quota_kb,
quota_messages)
        VALUES (18, 3, 'myname', MD5('PASSWORD_HERE'), 1000000,
1000000);
INSERT INTO virtual_users (id, domain_id, user, password, quota_kb,
quota_messages)
        VALUES (19, 3, 'contact', MD5('PASSWORD_HERE'), 1000000,
1000000);
INSERT INTO virtual_users (id, domain_id, user, password, quota_kb,
quota_messages)
        VALUES (20, 3, 'noreply', MD5('PASSWORD_HERE'), 1000000,
1000000);

INSERT INTO virtual_aliases (id, domain_id, source, destination)
```

VALUES (1, 5, 'root', 'aestudio@aestudio.sytes.net'),
(2, 1, 'root', 'repository@gmail.com'),
(3, 1, 'postmaster', 'aestudio@aestudio.sytes.net'),
(4, 1, 'xcapncrunchx', 'aestudio@aestudio.sytes.net'),
(5, 1, 'webmaster', 'aestudio@aestudio.sytes.net'),
(6, 1, 'lev', 'stv@gmail.com'),
(7, 1, 'myname', 'aestudio@aestudio.sytes.net'),
(8, 1, 'contact', 'aestudio@aestudio.sytes.net'),
(9, 1, 'noreply', 'aestudio@aestudio.sytes.net'),
(10, 4, 'webmaster', 'hereisthedeal@hereisthedeal.hopto.org'),
(11, 4, 'myname', 'hereisthedeal@hereisthedeal.hopto.org'),
(12, 4, 'contact', 'hereisthedeal@hereisthedeal.hopto.org'),
(13, 4, 'noreply', 'hereisthedeal@hereisthedeal.hopto.org'),
(14, 3, 'webmaster', 'etribe@etribe.sytes.net'),
(15, 3, 'myname', 'etribe@etribe.sytes.net'),
(16, 3, 'contact', 'etribe@etribe.sytes.net'),
(17, 3, 'noreply', 'etribe@etribe.sytes.net');

```
/* ---------------------------------------
      /home/aestudio/public_html/info.php
--------------------------------------- */
<?php phpinfo(); ?>


/* ---------------------------------------
      /home/xcapncrunchx/rsync-procedure
--------------------------------------- */
```

Create directories tosync under x1 and x2, and make 2 files under x2:

```
$ cd
$ mkdir tosync
$ cd tosync
```

On x2:

```
$ echo 'file-x2-1' > file-x2-1.txt
$ echo 'file-x2-2' > file-x2-2.txt
```

Command Template: How do I backup /var/www/html using rsync?
Resource:
http://www.cyberciti.biz/faq/noninteractive-shell-script-ssh-password-provider/
Run rsync over SSH using password authentication, passing the password on the command line:

```
$ rsync --rsh="sshpass -p myPassword ssh -l username" server.example.com:/var/www/html/ /backup/
```

NOTE: The first execution the command will not work if host were not connected for a first time
throuhg sh for that user, so:
As user on x1:
ssh x2
And then say yes to connect
No you can run the rsync with ssh commands

As user on x2:
ssh x1
And then say yes to connect
No you can run the rsync with ssh commands

To copy, running command from x1 the content of tosync on x2 to relative path in x1:
$ pass="ROOT-PASS_HERE"
$ rsync   -avv   --rsh="sshpass   -p $pass   ssh"
x2:/home/xcapncrunchx/tosync/ .

To include the directory tosync/ (DO NOT use the "/" symbol):
$ pass="ROOT-PASS_HERE"
$ rsync -avv --rsh="sshpass -p $pass ssh" x2:/home/xcapncrunchx/tosync
.
$ ls

Sync deleted files on origin to destiny (host):
$ pass="ROOT-PASS_HERE"
$ rsync   -avv   --delete   --rsh="sshpass   -p $pass   ssh"
x2:/home/xcapncrunchx/tosync/ .
$ ls

Sync just single file:
$ pass="ROOT-PASS_HERE"
$ rsync   -avv   --rsh="sshpass   -p $pass   ssh"
x2:/home/xcapncrunchx/tosync/file.txt .

RULE OF THUMB:
Take care that if you modify a file on destiny (for example x1) and synchronize from origin (x2)
you can lost changes made on destiny. so the rule of thumb is to always

181

make changes to sync on the
origin and call the sync command from destiny or destinies.

(READY)
Next step is test rsync using root:

Deactivate restriction to ssh as root:
$ sudo cp -dpR /etc/ssh_config /etc/ssh_configBAK3
$ sudo vim /etc/ssh_config

Rememmber to ssh the remote host from the destiny host (x1 to x2 and x2
to x1) to make
initial connection.

```perl
/* --------------------------------------------
     /home/xcapncrunchx/db_tables_sizing.pl
-------------------------------------------- */
```

Nota: Este archivo fue creado por usuarios de la comunidad de MySQL Cluster y adaptado por mí para LE SF.

```perl
#!/usr/bin/perl
use strict;
$| = 1;

my %DataType = (
"TINYINT"=>1, "SMALLINT"=>2, "MEDIUMINT"=>3, "INT"=>4,
"INTEGER"=>4, "BIGINT"=>8,
"FLOAT"=>'$M<=24?4:8', "DOUBLE"=>8,
"DECIMAL"=>'int(($M-$D)/9)*4+int(((($M-
$D)%9)+1)/2)+int($D/9)*4+int((($D%9)+1)/2)',
"NUMERIC"=>'int(($M-$D)/9)*4+int(((($M-
$D)%9)+1)/2)+int($D/9)*4+int((($D%9)+1)/2)',
"BIT"=>'($M+7)>>3',
"DATE"=>3, "TIME"=>3, "DATETIME"=>8, "TIMESTAMP"=>4,
"YEAR"=>1,
"BINARY"=>'$M',"CHAR"=>'$M*$CL',
"VARBINARY"=>'$M+($M>255?2:1)',
"VARCHAR"=>'$M*$CL+($M>255?2:1)',
"ENUM"=>'$M>255?2:1', "SET"=>'($M+7)>>3',
"TINYBLOB"=>9, "TINYTEXT"=>9,
"BLOB"=>10, "TEXT"=>10,
"MEDIUMBLOB"=>11, "MEDIUMTEXT"=>11,
"LONGBLOB"=>12, "LONGTEXT"=>12
);
```

```perl
my %DataTypeMin = (
"VARBINARY"=>'($M>255?2:1)', "VARCHAR"=>'($M>255?2:1)'
);

my ($D, $M, $S, $C, $L, $dt, $dp ,$bc, $CL);
my $fieldCount = 0;
my $byteCount = 0;
my $byteCountMin = 0;
my @fields = ();
my $fieldName;
my $tableName;
my $defaultDbCL = 1;
my $defaultTableCL = 1;
my %charsetMaxLen;
my %collationMaxLen;

open (CHARSETS, "mysql -B --skip-column-names information_schema -
p      -e 'select    CHARACTER_SET_NAME,MAXLEN    from
CHARACTER_SETS;' |");
%charsetMaxLen = map ( ( /^(\w+)/ => /(\d+)$/ ), <CHARSETS>);
close CHARSETS;

open    (COLLATIONS,    "mysql    -B    --skip-column-names
information_schema -p -e 'select COLLATION_NAME,MAXLEN from
CHARACTER_SETS      INNER      JOIN      COLLATIONS
USING(CHARACTER_SET_NAME);' |");
%collationMaxLen  =  map  (  (  /^(\w+)/  =>  /(\d+)$/  ),
<COLLATIONS>);
close COLLATIONS;

open (TABLEINFO, "mysqldump -d -p --compact ".join(" ",@ARGV)."
|");

while (<TABLEINFO>) {
 chomp;
 if             (        ($S,$C)           =       /create
database.*?`([^`]+)`.*default\scharacter\sset\s+(\w+)/i) {
 $defaultDbCL = exists $charsetMaxLen{$C} ? $charsetMaxLen{$C} : 1;
 print "Database: $S".($C?" DEFAULT":"").($C?" CHARSET $C":"")."
(bytes per char: $defaultDbCL)\n\n";
 next;
 }
```

```perl
if ( /^create table\s+`([^`]+)`.*/i ) {
$tableName = $1;
@fields = ();
next;
}
if ( $tableName && (($C,$L) =
/^\)(?:.*?default\scharset=(\w+))?(?:.*?collate=(\w+))?/i) ) {
$defaultTableCL = exists $charsetMaxLen{$C} ? $charsetMaxLen{$C} :
(exists $collationMaxLen{$L} ? $collationMaxLen{$L} : $defaultDbCL);
print "Table: $tableName".($C||$L?" DEFAULT":"").($C?" CHARSET
$C":"").($L?" COLLATION $L":"")." (bytes per char:
$defaultTableCL)\n";
$tableName = "";
$fieldCount = 0;
$byteCount = 0;
$byteCountMin = 0;
while ($_ = shift @fields) {
if ( ($fieldName,$dt,$dp,$M,$D,$S,$C,$L) = /\s\s`([^`]+)`\s+([a-
z]+)(\((\d+)(?:,(\d+))?\)|\((.*)\))?(?:.*?character\sset\s+(\w+))?(?:.*?colla
te\s+(\w+))?/i ) {
$dt = uc $dt;
if (exists $DataType{$dt}) {
if (length $S) {
$M = ($S =~ s/(\'.*?\'(?!\')(?=,|$))/$1/g);
$dp = "($M : $S)"
}
$D = 0 if !$D;
$CL = exists $charsetMaxLen{$C} ? $charsetMaxLen{$C} : (exists
$collationMaxLen{$L} ? $collationMaxLen{$L} : $defaultTableCL);
$bc = eval($DataType{$dt});
$byteCount += $bc;
$byteCountMin += exists $DataTypeMin{$dt} ? $DataTypeMin{$dt} :
$bc;
} else {
$bc = "??";
}
$fieldName.="\t" if length($fieldName) < 8;
print "bytes:\t".$bc."\t$fieldName\t$dt$dp".($C?" $C":"").($L?" COLL
$L":"")."\n";
++$fieldCount;
}
}
print "total:\t$byteCount".($byteCountMin!=$byteCount?"\tleast:
```

```
$byteCountMin":"\t\t")."\tcolumns: $fieldCount\n\n";
 next;
 }
 push @fields, $_;
 }
 close TABLEINFO;

/* --------------------------------
      /home/xcapncrunchx/awstats.sh
------------------------------- */
#!/bin/sh
# Updates the web sites visitors stats, based in the site log file in
/var/log/apache2/site-name.

# Perl script + Site config file list (/etc/awstats, no awstats preffix
# no conf suffix)
/usr/lib/cgi-bin/awstats.pl -config=aestudio
# /usr/lib/cgi-bin/awstats.pl -config=cronos.sytes.net
/usr/lib/cgi-bin/awstats.pl -config=etribe
/usr/lib/cgi-bin/awstats.pl -config=hereisthedeal


# Add new sites here



# Updates static stats in the tmp/awstats dir of every site,
# like /home/aestudio/tmp/awstats/*

# Update on 2/22/2012: After the processors speed and charge review,
decided to comment the next static pages perl scripts:

#/usr/share/doc/awstats/examples/awstats_buildstaticpages.pl -update -
config=aestudio          -dir=/home/aestudio/tmp/awstats/          -
awstatsprog=/usr/lib/cgi-bin/awstats.pl

# /usr/share/doc/awstats/examples/awstats_buildstaticpages.pl -update -
config=cronos.sytes.net        -dir=/home/web2/tmp/awstats/          -
awstatsprog=/usr/lib/cgi-bin/awstats.pl

# /usr/share/doc/awstats/examples/awstats_buildstaticpages.pl -update -
config=etribe          -dir=/home/etribe/tmp/awstats/          -
awstatsprog=/usr/lib/cgi-bin/awstats.pl
```

```
# /usr/share/doc/awstats/examples/awstats_buildstaticpages.pl -update -
config=hereisthedeal      -dir=/home/hereisthedeal/tmp/awstats/      -
awstatsprog=/usr/lib/cgi-bin/awstats.pl
```

```
/* ---------------------------------------
    /home/xcapncrunchx/Balance-push.sh
--------------------------------------- */
```

Nota: Este archivo se publicó en el libro Linux Server Hacks 100
Industrial-Strength Tips and Tools, por Rob Flickenger, de la editorial
O'Reilly® Associates, Inc. La version pública se puede obtener de Internet.
La presente versión es una adaptación para LE SF. En realidad se mantiene
una copia de su última versión en el espacio de usuario pero se ejecuta
como cron job que se puede observar en /etc/crontab y su verdadera
localización y la de sus archivos es /etc/balance/.

```
#!/bin/sh

#
#balance-push - Push content from the master server (localhost)
# to multiple front- and back-end servers, in parallel.
#

# $FRONT_END lists the servers that receive the front-end (e.g. static
content) updates.
#
FRONT_END=$(cat /etc/balance/servers.front)

# $BACK_END lists the hosts that receive the full back-end (e.g.
everything) updates.
#
BACK_END=$(cat /etc/balance/servers.back)

# $TARGET specifies the filesystem root on the remote host to push to.
# Normally, you want this to be /, unless you're doing testing.
#
TARGET=/

# $EXCLUDE specifies the prefix of the per-mode rsync exclude files.
# For example, if your exclude files are /usr/local/etc/balance.front and
# /usr/local/etc/balance.back, set this to "/usr/local/etc/balance". The
# per-mode extensions will be added.
#
EXCLUDE=/etc/balance/balance
```

```
# $LOCK_DIR specifies a path to put the lock files in.
#
LOCK_DIR=/var/tmp

######### Ignore the shell functions behind the curtain. #########

PATH=/bin:/usr/bin:/usr/local/bin

lock ( ) {
local lockfile="$LOCK_DIR/balance.$1.lock"
if [ -f $lockfile ]; then
if kill -0 $(cat $lockfile); then
echo "$0 appears to be already running on $1."
echo "Please check $lockfile if you think this is in error."
exit 1
else
echo "$0 appears to have completed for $1 without cleaning up its lockfile."
fi
fi
echo $$ > $lockfile
}

unlock ( ) {
rm -f $LOCK_DIR/balance.$1.lock
}

push_files ( ) {
local mode=$1 host=$2

if [ ! "$mode" -o ! -r "$EXCLUDE.$mode" ]; then
echo "$0 $$: mode unset for $host!"
return
fi

if [ ! "$host" ]; then
echo "$0 $$: host unset for push $mode!"
return
fi

lock $host
```

```
PASS=$(cat /etc/balance/pass)

#echo "$host: I am host"
#echo "${TARGET}: I am TARGET"
#echo "$mode: I am mode"
#echo "$EXCLUDE.$mode: I am EXCLUDE.mode"


rsync -avv --ignore-errors --whole-file --rsh="sshpass -p $PASS ssh" \
--exclude-from="$EXCLUDE.$mode" / ${host}:${TARGET}


# Test
#rsync -avv --delete --ignore-errors --whole-file --rsh="sshpass -p $PASS
ssh" / ${host}:${TARGET}

# Example command
#rsync --archive --rsh=ssh --delete --ignore-errors --whole-file \
#--exclude-from="$EXCLUDE.$mode" / ${host}:${TARGET}

#Example from my previous product video lessons
#rsync      -avv     --delete     --rsh="sshpass     -p     $PASS     ssh"
x2:/home/xcapncrunchx/tosync/ .


unlock $host
}

push_tier ( ) {
local mode=$1 host_list=$2

for host in $host_list; do
$SHELL -c "push_files $mode $host" &
done
}

export -f lock unlock push_files
export TARGET EXCLUDE LOCK_DIR PATH

[ "$FRONT_END" ] && push_tier front "$FRONT_END"
[ "$BACK_END" ] && push_tier back "$BACK_END"

#
```

```
# Fin.
#

/* ----------------------------------------
        /home/xcapncrunchx/balance.frontBAK
---------------------------------------- */
- aquota.group
- aquota.user
- bin/*
- boot/*
- cdrom
- dev/*
- etc/*
- fsck
- home/aquota.group
- home/aquota.user
- home/ftp2/*
- home/ftpBAK/*
- home/lost+found/*
- home/mycluster/*
- home/my_cluster/*
- home/ssh-agent/*
- home/web/*
- home/web1/*
- home/web2/*
- home/xcapncrunchx/*
- initrd/*
- initrd.img
- initrd.img.old
- lib/*
- lost+found/*
- media/*
- mnt/*
- opt
- proc/*
- root/*
- sbin/*
- selinux/*
- srv/*
- sys/*
- tmp/*
- usr/*
- var/*
```

- vmlinuz
- vmlinuz.old

```
/* ------------------------------------
      /home/xcapncrunchx/balance.front
------------------------------------ */
```
- aquota.group
- aquota.user
- bin/*
- boot/*
- cdrom
- dev/*
- etc/*
- fsck
- home/aquota.group
- home/aquota.user
- home/ftp2/*
- home/ftpBAK/*
- home/lost+found/*
- home/mycluster/*
- home/my_cluster/*
- home/ssh-agent/*
- home/web/*
- home/web1/*
- home/web2/*
- home/xcapncrunchx/*
- initrd/*
- initrd.img
- initrd.img.old
- lib/*
- lost+found/*
- media/*
- mnt/*
- opt
- proc/*
- root/*
- sbin/*
- selinux/*
- srv/*
- sys/*
- tmp/*
- usr/*
- var/aquota.group

- var/aquota.user
- var/backups/*
- var/cache/*
- var/lib/amavis/*
- var/lib/apt/*
- var/lib/aptitude/*
- var/lib/awstats/*
- var/lib/clamav/*
- var/lib/clamav-data/*
- var/lib/defoma/*
- var/lib/dhcp/*
- var/lib/dhcp3/*
- var/lib/dictionaries-common/*
- var/lib/dovecot/*
- var/lib/dpkg/*
- var/lib/exim4/*
- var/lib/initramfs-tools/*
- var/lib/initscripts/*
- var/lib/libuuid/*
- var/lib/logrotate/*
- var/lib/misc/*
- var/lib/mysql/ALL
- var/lib/mysql/clusterdb/*
- var/lib/mysql/comic_book_app/*
- var/lib/mysql/debian-5.0.flag
- var/lib/mysql/galaxydb/*
- var/lib/mysql/ibdata1
- var/lib/mysql/ib_logfile0
- var/lib/mysql/ib_logfile1
- var/lib/mysql/lescifi/*
- var/lib/mysql/moondb/*
- var/lib/mysql/mysql/*
- var/lib/mysql/mysql_upgrade_info
- var/lib/mysql/sundb/*
- var/lib/mysql/web_development/*
- var/lib/mysql-cluster/*
- var/lib/nfs/*
- var/lib/noip2/*
- var/lib/ntp/*
- var/lib/ntpdate/*
- var/lib/php5/*
- var/lib/phpmyadmin/*
- var/lib/postfix/*

- var/lib/pycentral/*
- var/lib/python-sepolgen/*
- var/lib/python-support
- var/lib/quota/*
- var/lib/sepolgen/*
- var/lib/sgml-base/*
- var/lib/squirrelmail/*
- var/lib/sudo/*
- var/lib/tex-common/*
- var/lib/tripwire/*
- var/lib/ucf/*
- var/lib/urandom/*
- var/lib/usbutils/*
- var/lib/vim/*
- var/lib/x11/*
- var/lib/xml-core/*
- var/local/*
- var/lock/*
- var/log/*
- var/lost+found/*
- var/mail/*
- var/opt/*
- var/run/*
- var/spool/*
- var/tmp/*
- var/www/*
- vmlinuz
- vmlinuz.old

```
/* -----------------------------------
      /home/xcapncrunchx/balance.back
----------------------------------- */
```

- aquota.group
- aquota.user
- bin/*
- boot/*
- cdrom
- dev/*
- etc/*
- fsck
- home/*
- initrd/*
- initrd.img

- initrd.img.old
- lib/*
- lost+found/*
- media/*
- mnt/*
- opt
- proc/*
- root/*
- sbin/*
- selinux/*
- srv/*
- sys/*
- tmp/*
- usr/*
- var/*
- vmlinuz
- vmlinuz.old

```
/* ------------------------------------
        /home/xcapncrunchx/servers.front
------------------------------------- */
x1
```

```
/* ----------------------------------
        /home/xcapncrunchx/servers.back
-------------------------------------- */
```

Nota: Se ha dejado este archivo en blanco para el proyecto Linux Enterprise Sci Fi, sin embargo podría llegar a utilizarse dependiendo del diseño del ambiente y sus sistemas.

```
/* ----------------------------------------------
        /home/xcapncrunchx/bastion-server-firewall.sh
---------------------------------------------- */
```

Nota: Este archivo contiene porciones de scripts de firewall de los libros: Linux Server Security, por Michael D. Bauer, de Editorial O'Reilly® Media Inc, y SuSE Linux 7.2 Network, por varios autores, de Editorial SuSE GmbH. Fue creado por su servidor para LE SF.

```
#! /bin/sh
# System startup script for local packet filters on a bastion server
# in a DMZ (NOT for an actual firewall)
# Created by Esteban Herrera.

# Useful iptables commands to debugging rule's time:
```

```
# Shows the rules' table:
#iptables -L

# Shows the rules's table, giving a consecutive number to each rule:
#iptables -L -n --line

# Eliminate one rule by its consecutive number (e.g.: "1"):
#iptables -D INPUT 1

# Flush active rules and custom tables (for me including the tables of the
program fail2ban.
# Stops the firewall. The system will need some rules.
# Notice: iptables -F = iptables --flush
#iptables --flush
#iptables --delete-chain

# Secuence to a wide open firewall, used, for example, after a wrong setup:
#iptables --flush
#iptables -P INPUT ACCEPT
#iptables -P FORWARD ACCEPT
#iptables -P OUTPUT ACCEPT

# Querying iptables status
#iptables --line-numbers -v --list

# Modules required by the specified module.
# (The other way to up modules at startup is to add them to /etc/modules.
With 'modprobe'
# every module is up with the correspondent modules as dependencies. To
list modules use 'lsmod'.
modprobe ip_tables
modprobe ip_conntrack_ftp

# Flush active rules and custom tables
# Next commands are specifically applied to do not touch the fail2ban
custom chains,
# See 'man i[ptables' for details:
iptables --flush -t nat
# iptables --flush -t filter
# iptables --delete-chain

# Set default-deny policies for all three default chains
```

```
iptables -P INPUT DROP
iptables -P FORWARD DROP
iptables -P OUTPUT DROP
```

```
# Give free reign to the loopback interfaces, i.e. local processes may connect
# to other processes' listening-ports.
iptables -A INPUT  -i lo -j ACCEPT
iptables -A OUTPUT -o lo -j ACCEPT
```

```
# Do some rudimentary anti-IP-spoofing drops. The rule of thumb is "drop
# any source IP address which is impossible" (per RFC 1918)
#
# NOTE: If you use RFC 1918 address-space, comment out or edit the appropriate
# lines below!
#
iptables -A INPUT -s 255.0.0.0/8 -j LOG --log-prefix "Spoofed source IP"
iptables -A INPUT -s 255.0.0.0/8 -j DROP
iptables -A INPUT -s 0.0.0.0/8 -j LOG --log-prefix "Spoofed source IP"
iptables -A INPUT -s 0.0.0.0/8 -j DROP
iptables -A INPUT -s 127.0.0.0/8 -j LOG --log-prefix "Spoofed source IP"
iptables -A INPUT -s 127.0.0.0/8 -j DROP
# The local IP of my server is 192.168.1.6, so activating next 2 lines the mail
# server (squirrelmail Front end) does not connect to localhost (IMAP)!
#iptables -A INPUT -s 192.168.0.0/16 -j LOG --log-prefix "Spoofed source IP"
#iptables -A INPUT -s 192.168.0.0/16 -j DROP
iptables -A INPUT -s 172.16.0.0/12 -j LOG --log-prefix "Spoofed source IP"
iptables -A INPUT -s 172.16.0.0/12 -j DROP
iptables -A INPUT -s 10.0.0.0/8 -j LOG --log-prefix " Spoofed source IP"
iptables -A INPUT -s 10.0.0.0/8 -j DROP
```

```
# Commands to help debugging software installation:
# To list open ports (services are named under /etc/services):
#netstat -plunt
#netstat -plunt | grep 123
# To scan from remote host open ports (services listening for new requests only, no client
# ports):
```

#nmap -O remote_host
Scan specific ports (Client ports like 123 will appear as closed):
#nmap -p 1186 x1
#nmap -p 123 x1
Port tool http://www.canyouseeme.org/
Check network, i.e. DNS, Gateway, proxy
Check router DMZ and configuration

In this section we will add the list of IP CONFLICTIVE addresses that attacked
us for example with DDOS or Brute Force, problems not resolved with something
like apache mod evasive.

Useful commands at combat time versus attackers:
#netstat -nr [Kernel ip routing table].
#netstat .inet -aln [See all the active sockets of ports].
#netstat -tap [Verify connection, for example, open ports of the server].
#netstat -i [Displays the configuredinterfaces].
#netstat -ia [Displays all the interfaces].
#netstat -ta [Displays the active TCP connections, with the ports in LISTEN state].
When we are being attacked, an excellent way to discover the requests to
the 80 port by IP is (as root):
#netstat -plan|grep :80 | awk {'print $5'}|cut -d: -f 1|sort|uniq -c|sort -n
Other 'netstat' command will tell what are IPs with established connections:
#netstat -plan|grep :80 | grep ESTABLISHED | awk {'print $5'}|cut -d: -f 1|sort|uniq -c|sort -n
Both commands will help us to recognize what IP (or IPs) is (or are) exceeding the max permitted
requests' quantity (when the attack is on port ":80").
The next step is to filter the address is giving problems, for example using the 'APF' program
'sh> /usr/local/sbin/apf -d <IP conflictive>'.
#traceroute -n www.google.com [Verifies routes and connectivity].
#traceroute -i 208.67.222.222 [Verifies routes but and connectivity but using ICMP (Internet
Control Message Protocol) messages].
#mtr .-psize 1024 208.67.222.222 [Verifies. An option to traceroute command but with more
displays. This example is using the DNS for cronos, the DNS assigning
#arp -e [Verify the arp tables].

Install the nmap sniffer with 'apt-get update', then type 'apt-get install nmap'.
#nmap {-s scanningKind} {-p portsRange} -F options objective [nmap scanner syntax].
#nmap -sT -F -P0 -O woofgang.dogpeople.org   [Probing   iptables and a strong system].
#nmap -sTUR -F -P0 -O woofgang.dogpeople.org   [A   more detailed port scanning].
#nmap -sP 192.168.0.0/24 [Sniff a network].
If can't identify intruder install snort, a network intrusion prevention and detection system
(IDS/IPS). For more info visit: http://www.snort.org.
More here...

Consider next line to insert, in real time, the attacker IP address, in the command line
Then, if needed you will add the address ro thte blacklist below. THis will help
when we can't stop the active connections in the firewall because of the natures of the rules
where all is DROPPED by default. The '-I' part of the command means "insert", and the
the number '1' tells the new rule line will be inserted before the rule number '1'.
Before any insertion verify the rule numbers to the INPUT chain, and be carefull:

#iptables -I INPUT 1 -s 192.168.1.4 -j LOG --log-prefix "Potential RT DoS src IP"
#iptables -I INPUT 1 -s 192.168.1.4 -j DROP

In this way we are not going to accept incoming requests (inputs) from MyBlackList addresses:
In the next example, a local client with a local ip.

#iptables -A INPUT -s 192.168.1.4 -j LOG --log-prefix "Potential DoS source IP"
#iptables -A INPUT -s 192.168.1.4 -j DROP

The following will NOT interfere with local inter-process traffic, whose
packets have the source IP of the local loopback interface, e.g. 127.0.0.1
(The source is our IP [$IP_LOCAL] , so it is false.

iptables -A INPUT -s 201.201.101.162 -j LOG --log-prefix "Spoofed source myIP"
iptables -A INPUT -s 201.201.101.162 -j DROP

Tell netfilter that all TCP sessions do indeed begin with SYN
(There may be some RFC-non-compliant application somewhere which
begins its transactions otherwise, but if so I've never heard of it)

iptables -A INPUT -p tcp ! --syn -m state --state NEW -j LOG --log-prefix "Stealth scan attempt?"
iptables -A INPUT -p tcp ! --syn -m state --state NEW -j DROP

Finally, the meat of our packet-filtering policy:

INBOUND POLICY
(Applies to packets entering our network interface from the network,
and addressed to this host)

Useful List of ports:
<<< Ports to open list (the complete list in on the file /etc/services): >>>
Search services with: 'sh> cat /etc/services/ | grep http | grep tcp' (for http ports info).
80   > http
443   > https
21   > ftp
115   > sftp
25   > smtp
110   > Pop3
???   > pop3S
143   > IMAP
993   > IMAPs
????   > Java (apache tomcat)
????   > C# (asp, like :8083)
more ...
#
<<< Do not open list, but maybe necessary for the server administration (from my notebook): >>>
#

??? > NFS (Avoid it or only let it be local)

8222 > Tomcat http VMware® (not needed is on foobar (192.168.1.4))

8333 > Tomcat https VMware® (not needed is on foobar (192.168.1.4))

22 > ssh default port

???? > ssh changed to other port higher than the port 1024.

23 > telnet (had to be explicitly denied using netfilter rules. Can be used to connect to other port,

for example 'sh> telnet 192.168.1.6 80', then type 'HEAD' and press ENTER key)

10024 > amavis listening for postfix mail (open not needed, the loopback has free reign)

10025 > postfix listening amavis mail (open not needed, loopback has free reign)

Remote Desktop > 3389

5900 > Real VNC

PC Anywhere > 5631

3306 > mysql. PHPMyAdmin uses 3306 and is not affected. MYSQL server in other machine needs both ports open.

???? > ICMP (The Internet Control Messaging Proto, for Internet equip communication. Includes:

server, router, etc.

The port can be open periodically (in ms) in order to help costumers to find,

for example a web server. Setup this in other script file). That script will

help with other script that do ping to a place, also periodically,

to maintain open the Internet connection's portished against DOS attacks and bottlenecks,

but i don't need that script, my router comes with a check to the anti DOS attacks

integrated option, out of the box. Anyway enforce in the firewall and every machine with

hardware and software is always the best decision to forge the knight's shield.

873 > rsync. Maybe required for the ftp-backup server.

992 > telnets. Secure telnet.

2049 > NFS. Port for Net File System, require to make grow the /var partition.

3690 > svn.

5060 > sip.

5061 > sip-tls.

5190 > aol.

1194 > openvpn.

194   > irc.
more...

Accept inbound packets that are part of previously-OK'ed sessions
iptables -A INPUT -m state --state RELATED,ESTABLISHED -j ACCEPT

SERVER AND HOST CLUSTER RULES:

Accept inbound packets which initiate SSH sessions
Remeber the default and changed ports
#iptables -A INPUT -p tcp -j ACCEPT --dport 22 -m state --state NEW
#iptables -A INPUT -p tcp -j ACCEPT --dport 49 -m state --state NEW
--== Next line changed to limit to a local host access the server through ssh.==--
The address can be an Intranet firewall (with static IP), facing the bastion server behind the DMZ.
#iptables -A INPUT -p tcp -j ACCEPT -s 192.168.1.10 --dport 49 -m state --state NEW
--== Next are activated to preserve the local host address (e.g. my notebook) like dynamic
where my notebook ip change sometimes in a network of 5 computers, the router is configured
to give dynamic IPs beginning from 192.168.1.10 ==--
#iptables -A INPUT -p tcp -j ACCEPT -s 192.168.1.10 --dport 49 -m state --state NEW
#iptables -A INPUT -p tcp -j ACCEPT -s 192.168.1.11 --dport 49 -m state --state NEW
#iptables -A INPUT -p tcp -j ACCEPT -s 192.168.1.12 --dport 49 -m state --state NEW
#iptables -A INPUT -p tcp -j ACCEPT -s 192.168.1.13 --dport 49 -m state --state NEW
#iptables -A INPUT -p tcp -j ACCEPT -s 192.168.1.14 --dport 49 -m state --state NEW

--== Next is the template just in case we need more open, for a specific host ==--
#iptables -A INPUT -p tcp -j ACCEPT -s 192.168.1.10 --dport 49 -m state --state NEW

To Accept packets from trusted network:
#iptables -A INPUT -s 192.168.0.0/24 -j ACCEPT # using standard slash notation

#iptables -A INPUT -s 192.168.0.0/255.255.255.0 -j ACCEPT # using a subnet mask

Accept inbound packets which initiate ssh sessions from hosts in the network 192.168.1.0,
which is supposed to be the local cluster network (I.E: hosts named x1, x2, foobar, vgui).
iptables -A INPUT -s 192.168.1.0/255.255.255.0 -p tcp -j ACCEPT --dport 22 -m state --state NEW

To Accept packets from trusted IP addresses, for client hosts with many active ethernet interfaces,
It's not the ssh client that decides through which interface TCP packets should go (to reach a server
behind a firewall like this), it's the kernel. In short, SSH asks the kernel to open a connection to
a certain IP address, and the kernel decides which interface is to be used by consulting the routing
tables. In this case you will have to add one policy for every ethernet IP in the host. Also, you can
display the kernel routing tables with the commands route -n and/or ip route show and perhaps modify
temporarily (or with a script) the route table to match your needs.
Use this policy to connect to remote cluster hosts public IPs (I.E: y1, y2, foobar2, and a remote
vgui). Otherwise I will have to leave ssh port wide open to the Internet to reach cluster servers.
#iptables   -A   INPUT   -s   192.168.0.4   -m   mac   --mac-source 00:50:8D:FD:E6:32 -j ACCEPT

Accept inbound packets which initiate NTP (Network Time Protocol) sessions
iptables -A INPUT -p tcp -j ACCEPT --dport 123 -m state --state NEW

Accept inbound packets which initiate MySQL Cluster sessions
iptables -A INPUT -p tcp -j ACCEPT --dport 1186 -m state --state NEW

USER SERVICES RULES:

Accept inbound packets which initiate FTP sessions
iptables -A INPUT -p tcp -j ACCEPT --dport 21 -m state --state NEW

--= Next new lines are specific for FTP, if you have troubles with the

FTP passive mode. For the most of configurations it is only necessary
the installation of the module ftp-conntrack, put the rules in the the headers of the chains
INPUT and OUTPUT, and finally establish the rules to the INPUT chain to let be new connections
in the TCP port 21. If that does not work, use 2 lines here: ==--

#iptables -A INPUT -p tcp --sport 1024: --dport 1024: -m state --state ESTABLISHED -j ACCEPT
#iptables -A OUTPUT -p tcp --sport 1024: --dport 1024: -m state --state ESTABLISHED,RELATED -j ACCEPT

Accept inbound packets which initiate HTTP sessions
iptables -A INPUT -p tcp -j ACCEPT --dport 80 -m state --state NEW

Accept inbound packets which initiate HTTPS sessions
iptables -A INPUT -p tcp -j ACCEPT --dport 443 -m state --state NEW

Accept inbound packets which initiate IMAP sessions
iptables -A INPUT -p tcp -j ACCEPT --dport 143 -m state --state NEW

Accept inbound packets which initiate IMAP3 sessions
iptables -A INPUT -p tcp -j ACCEPT --dport 220 -m state --state NEW

Accept inbound packets which initiate IMAPS sessions
iptables -A INPUT -p tcp -j ACCEPT --dport 993 -m state --state NEW

Accept inbound packets which initiate POP2 sessions
iptables -A INPUT -p tcp -j ACCEPT --dport 109 -m state --state NEW

Accept inbound packets which initiate POP3 sessions
iptables -A INPUT -p tcp -j ACCEPT --dport 110 -m state --state NEW

Accept inbound packets which initiate POP3S sessions
iptables -A INPUT -p tcp -j ACCEPT --dport 995 -m state --state NEW

Accept inbound packets which initiate SMTP sessions
iptables -A INPUT -p tcp -j ACCEPT --dport 25 -m state --state NEW

Accept inbound packets which initiate SSMTP sessions
iptables -A INPUT -p tcp -j ACCEPT --dport 465 -m state --state NEW

--== Next is the protocol template just in case we need more open to all

client hosts ==--
Accept inbound packets which initiate PROTOCOL-HERE sessions
#iptables -A INPUT -p tcp -j ACCEPT --dport 80 -m state --state NEW

Log and drop anything not accepted above
(Obviously we want to log any packet that doesn't match any ACCEPT rule, for
both security and troubleshooting. Note that the final "DROP" rule is
redundant if the default policy is already DROP, but redundant security is
usually a good thing.)
iptables -A INPUT -j LOG --log-prefix "Dropped by default (INPUT):"
iptables -A INPUT -j DROP

OUTBOUND POLICY
(Applies to packets sent to the network interface (NOT loopback)
from local processes)

If it's part of an approved connection, let it out
iptables -I OUTPUT 1 -m state --state RELATED,ESTABLISHED -j ACCEPT

Allow outbound ping
(For testing only! If someone compromises your system they may attempt
to use ping to identify other active IP addresses on the DMZ. Comment
this rule out when you don't need to use it yourself!)
#
#iptables -A OUTPUT -p icmp -j ACCEPT --icmp-type echo-request

Allow outbound DNS queries, e.g. to resolve IPs in logs
(Many network applications break or radically slow down if they
can't use DNS. Although DNS queries usually use UDP 53, they may also use TCP
53. Although TCP 53 is normally used for zone-transfers, DNS queries with
replies greater than 512 bytes also use TCP 53, so we'll allow both TCP and UDP
53 here
#
iptables -A OUTPUT -p udp --dport 53 -m state --state NEW -j ACCEPT
iptables -A OUTPUT -p tcp --dport 53 -m state --state NEW -j ACCEPT

SERVER AND HOST CLUSTER RULES:

All the ssh output is accepted:
Accept inbound packets which initiate ssh sessions from hosts in the network 192.168.1.0
iptables -A OUTPUT -p tcp --dport 22 -m state --state NEW -j ACCEPT

Accept inbound packets which initiate NTP (Network Time Protocol) sessions
iptables -A OUTPUT -p tcp --dport 123 -m state --state NEW -j ACCEPT

Accept inbound packets which initiate MySQL Cluster sessions
iptables -A OUTPUT -p tcp --dport 1186 -m state --state NEW -j ACCEPT

#---------- Mail service outs:

Accept inbound packets which initiate IMAP sessions
iptables -A OUTPUT -p tcp --dport 143 -m state --state NEW -j ACCEPT

Accept inbound packets which initiate IMAP3 sessions
iptables -A OUTPUT -p tcp --dport 220 -m state --state NEW -j ACCEPT

Accept inbound packets which initiate IMAPS sessions
iptables -A OUTPUT -p tcp --dport 993 -m state --state NEW -j ACCEPT

Accept inbound packets which initiate POP2 sessions
iptables -A OUTPUT -p tcp --dport 109 -m state --state NEW -j ACCEPT

Accept inbound packets which initiate POP3 sessions
iptables -A OUTPUT -p tcp --dport 110 -m state --state NEW -j ACCEPT

Accept inbound packets which initiate POP3S sessions
iptables -A OUTPUT -p tcp --dport 995 -m state --state NEW -j ACCEPT

Accept inbound packets which initiate SMTP sessions
iptables -A OUTPUT -p tcp --dport 25 -m state --state NEW -j ACCEPT

Accept inbound packets which initiate SSMTP sessions
iptables -A OUTPUT -p tcp --dport 465 -m state --state NEW -j ACCEPT

#------------

Log & drop anything not accepted above; if for no other reason, for troubleshooting
#
NOTE: you might consider setting your log-checker (e.g. Swatch) to
sound an alarm whenever this rule fires; unexpected outbound trans-
actions are often a sign of intruders!
#
iptables -A OUTPUT -j LOG --log-prefix "Dropped by default (OUTPUT):"
iptables -A OUTPUT -j DROP

Log & drop ALL incoming packets destined anywhere but here.
(We already set the default FORWARD policy to DROP. But this is
yet another free, reassuring redundancy, so why not throw it in?)
Attempted FWD? Dropped by default:
#
iptables -A FORWARD -j LOG --log-prefix "FWD Dropped by default:"
iptables -A FORWARD -j DROP

exit

```
/* --------------------------------------------------
      /home/xcapncrunchx/mysql-cluster-procedure.sh
-------------------------------------------------- */
!#/bin/sh
```

DANGER!:
> Do not use this script at system startup (as a rc service).
> You always must safely shutdown after the system login,
before you do anything else like re-add data-node
to the cluster, etc. Otherwise the server will delete the tables,
i.e.: (for table simples) simples.frm and simples.ndb under
/var/lib/mysql/clusterdb/ and your ndb-cluster databases will be lost.

MySQL Cluster procedure.

Use 'whereis + command' to find out the command executable location;

1. Check system health:

1.1 Check memory resources:

#swapon -s

```
#free
#ps -aux
#ps -aux | less
#top  (check processes of ndbd [1 per data node], ndb_mgmt and mysql
#df -h

# 1.2 Check services statuses:

#/etc/init.d/mysql status
# If you don't want to stop the service don't use next command, use
# management node status:
# /etc/init.d/mysql-ndb-mgm stop
# management node status:
#ndb_mgm -e show

# 2. Check logs and data directories:

# Command to check log files:
#less +F ndb_*.log
# To close the file use keys: CTRL + C and then press 'q' (quit).

# 2.1:

# 2.1.1: Directory defined in /etc/mysql/ndb_mgmd.cnf:

# datadir=/home/my_cluster/ndb_data

# 2.1.2: Directories where mysql-cluster sends the files if datadir option
# is not set:

# /
# /etc/init.d
# /etc/mysql/*
# /root
# /home/user_directory

# Example: List of Files and directories:

# CONFIG FILES:

# conf.d/
# config.ini
# debian.cnf
```

debian-start*
my.cnf
my.cnfBAK
my.cnfBAK2

NODE 1 (MGMT):

ndb_1_cluster.log (*)
ndb_1_out.log
ndb_1.pid

NODE 3 (DATA NODE):

ndb_3_error.log   (*)
ndb_3_fs/   (data files)
ndb_3_out.log   (*)
ndb_3.pid   (*)

(1 more every reboot without safely shutdown):

ndb_3_trace.log.1
ndb_3_trace.log.2
ndb_3_trace.log.3
ndb_3_trace.log.4
ndb_3_trace.log.5
ndb_3_trace.log.6
ndb_3_trace.log.next

NODE 4 (DATA NODE):

ndb_4_error.log   (*)
ndb_4_fs/   (data files)
ndb_4_out.log   (*)
ndb_4.pid   (*)

(1 more every reboot without safely shutdown):

ndb_4_trace.log.1
ndb_4_trace.log.2
ndb_4_trace.log.3
ndb_4_trace.log.4
ndb_4_trace.log.5
ndb_4_trace.log.6

ndb_4_trace.log.next

ndb_pid3425_error.log
ndb_pid3604_error.log
ndb_pid3606_error.log
ndb_pid3619_error.log
ndb_pid3620_error.log
ndb_pid4254_error.log

2.2 Mysql logs:
/var/log/mysql/*
/var/log/mysql.log

3. Check mysql databases directories:

/var/lib/mysql
/var/lib/mysql-cluster

4. Safely shutdown:

4.0: Back up the files db.opt simples.frm simples.ndb,
allocated under /var/lib/mysql/ndb-cluster-database_names or the complete
directory /var/lib/mysql/*, including non mysql-cluster databases.

4.1 The Debian way (use this!):

#/etc/init.d/mysql status (check status)
#/etc/init.d/mysql stop
#ndb_mgm -e show   (check status)
#/etc/init.d/mysql-ndb-mgm stop

4.2 Using mysql commands (mysql official documentation):

#/usr/bin/mysqladmin -u root2 -pPASSWORDSTRINGHERE -h 127.0.0.1 shutdown
Or with password prompt:
#/usr/bin/mysqladmin -u root2 -p -h 127.0.0.1 shutdown
#/usr/bin/ndb_mgm -e shutdown

5. Restart mysql cluster including new data nodes:

5.1 The Debian way (see sections 4.1 and 2.1. Use this!):

```
#/etc/init.d/mysql start
#/etc/init.d/mysql-ndb-mgm start

# Run this script data-nodes-start-up.sh to up the data nodes
# or run next nd-cluster command once per node in the file
# /etc/mysql/ndb_mgmd.cnf (Please add more data nodes to complete the
# existent amount):
/usr/sbin/ndbd -c localhost:1186
echo "Data node 3 seems to be up"
/usr/sbin/ndbd -c localhost:1186
echo "Data node 4 seems to be up"

# 5.2 Using mysql commands (mysql official documentation):

# (DANGER: The logfile group is created when the data nodes are started
# with --initial. Starting that data node with --initial causes all files
# in the directory to be deleted!). --initial is not working with
# next command (with debian binaries from apt sources) why?. If I use
# the command, the files will appear where the file (declared with
# the argument -f) is (see section 2.3 and choose option 5.1):
#/usr/sbin/ndb_mgmd -f /etc/mysql/ndb_mgmd.cnf
# Add one line per data-node in the file /etc/mysql/ndb_mgmd.cnf
#/usr/sbin/ndbd -c localhost:1186
#echo "Data node 3 seems to be up"
#/usr/sbin/ndbd -c localhost:1186
#echo "Data node 4 seems to be up"

# Restart mysql service:

#/etc/init.d/mysql stop
#/etc/init.d/mysql start
# or use:
#/etc/init.d/mysql restart

# 6. Check nodes show (and are) up:

#/usr/bin/ndb_mgm -e show
# or use the CLI (interface):
#ndb_mgm
#ndb_mgm> show
# To exit the CLI:
#ndb_mgm> exit
```

The output will show data nodes are connected, for example:

Connected to Management Server at: localhost:1186
Cluster Configuration

[ndbd(NDB)] 2 node(s)
id=3 @127.0.0.1 (mysql-5.5.19 ndb-7.2.4, Nodegroup: 0, Master)
id=4 @127.0.0.1 (mysql-5.5.19 ndb-7.2.4, Nodegroup: 0)
[ndb_mgmd(MGM)] 1 node(s)
id=1 @127.0.0.1 (mysql-5.5.19 ndb-7.2.4)
[mysqld(API)] 1 node(s)
id=50 (not connected, accepting connect from any host)

Sometimes mysql nodes appear as not connected but I you go to check
the new database with mysql, the manager will say to mysqld
"go and connect you!"

7. If the nodes are still down, restart this procedure from sections
"1. Check system health:" or "4.Safely shutdown:", depending on
the issue.

8. Check existent databases with phpmyadmin and Workbench.

9. Create a test database:

#mysql -h 127.0.0.1 -u root2 -p
Type password for mysql new user root2
We are in the mysql CLI:
#mysql> create database clusterdb;use clusterdb;
#mysql> create table simples (id int not null primary key) engine=ndb;
Note: All the ndbcluster tables need ID field)
#mysql> insert into simples values (1),(2),(3),(4);
#mysql> select * from simples;
Type 'exit' or 'quit' to return to the shell.

See new db under /var/lib/mysql
Check phmyadmin access to new db and table.
Check you can edit the table using Workbench.

10. Reboot the system.

Check the Virtual machine output is ok during startup.

11. Start mysql cluster according to section "5. Restart mysql
cluster including new data nodes:".

Run management node status:
ndb_mgm -e show

12. Confirm everything is going as expected:

Check again the new databases are OK. Check one db and one ndb-cluster
database at least.
exit

```
/* ------------------------------
      /home/xcapncrunchx/pen.sh
------------------------------ */
!#/bin/sh
### BEGIN INIT INFO
# Provides:       pen
# Required-Start: $local_fs $network
# Required-Stop:  $local_fs
# Default-Start:  2 3 4 5
# Default-Stop:   0 1 6
# Short-Description: pen
# Description:     pen loadbalancer and proxy daemon
### END INIT INFO
# Distribuites the workload between the servers in the cluster.
# -----------------------------------------------------------
# To Re-configure Pen in real time on the fly:
# A- Kill previous running Pen:
#ps -aux | grep pen
#kill <PID>
# B- Add a new Proxy rule:
#pen -r -a -d Load-balancer-IP:PORT>  <cluster-host-1-IP:PORT>
<cluster-host-n-IP:PORT> ...
# You can redirect from one port number in the loadbalancer to a another
port number
# in the cluster ( high availability )host.
# C- To limit the max amount of connections:
# Here three servers cooperate in a web server farm. Host www1 runs its
web server on
# port 8000 and accepts a maximum of 10 simultaneous connections.
```

Host www2
runs on port 80 and accepts 10 connections. Finally, www3 runs its web server on port
80 and allows an unlimited number of simultaneous connections.
#pen 80 www1:8000:10 www2:80:10 www3
D- To block all the connections by running a new pen command in mode FOREFRONT:
#pen -r -a -d -f Load-balancer-IP:PORT> <cluster-host-1-IP:PORT> <cluster-host-n-IP:PORT> ...

System boot up rules:
Update any changes on firewall scripts in the route like include
bastion-server-firewall.sh
Don't include port 22 which is for ssh because PEN will don't forward it.
Anyway we need this ports not forwarded to access the load balancer
through secure shell.
Ports list:
ntp: 123
MySQL Cluster: 1186
ftp: 21
http (web):   80
https (web):   443
imap: 143
imap3:   220
imaps: 993
pop2:   109
pop3:   110
pop3s: 995
smtp: 25
ssmtp: 465
...
pen -r -a 192.168.1.199:123 192.168.1.200:123 192.168.1.205:123
pen -r -a 192.168.1.199:1186 192.168.1.200:1186 192.168.1.205:1186
pen -r -a 192.168.1.199:21 192.168.1.200:21 192.168.1.205:21
pen -r -a 192.168.1.199:80 192.168.1.200:80 192.168.1.205:80
pen -r -a 192.168.1.199:443 192.168.1.200:443 192.168.1.205:443
pen -r -a 192.168.1.199:143 192.168.1.200:143 192.168.1.205:143
pen -r -a 192.168.1.199:220 192.168.1.200:220 192.168.1.205:220
pen -r -a 192.168.1.199:993 192.168.1.200:993 192.168.1.205:993
pen -r -a 192.168.1.199:109 192.168.1.200:109 192.168.1.205:109
pen -r -a 192.168.1.199:110 192.168.1.200:110 192.168.1.205:110
pen -r -a 192.168.1.199:995 192.168.1.200:995 192.168.1.205:995
pen -r -a 192.168.1.199:25 192.168.1.200:25 192.168.1.205:25

```
pen -r -a 192.168.1.199:465 192.168.1.200:465 192.168.1.205:465
#
#
# Once the balancers are up and running it's time to bind the virtual ip
# on the balancer's IP:
#sh /etc/init.d/pen-virtual-ip.sh

exit

/* ------------------------------------------
       /home/xcapncrunchx/pen-virtual-ip.sh
-------------------------------------------- */
!#/bin/sh
### BEGIN INIT INFO
# Provides:        dovecot
# Required-Start:  $local_fs $network
# Required-Stop:   $local_fs
# Default-Start:   2 3 4 5
# Default-Stop:    0 1 6
# Short-Description: dovecot
# Description:      dovecot pop & imap daemon
### END INIT INFO
# Bind host ip addresses set in eth0 to create virtual IP address
(192.168.1.197)
# Now try surfing to http://192.168.1.197/. One of the load balancers will
be active
# and respond at that address. Disconnect that load balancer from the
network to
# simulate a failure. Now the other load balancer will take over the address,
# restoring functionality.
# In the example network, the firewall uses NAT, although that is in no
way
# necessary. A Cisco PIX would be configured something like this:
# static (inside,outside) 193.12.6.25 10.1.1.4 netmask 255.255.255.255 0 0
# conduit permit tcp host 193.12.6.25 eq 80 any
vrrpd -i eth0 -v 1 192.168.1.197

exit

/* -----------------------------------
       /home/xcapncrunchx/tripwire.sh
------------------------------------ */
#!/bin/sh
```

```
# Generating new tripwire report file to /var/lib/tripwire/report/*
including a
# date time stamp and the extension .twr to it.

tripwire --check
# when active, next line can send reports via email to the users added in
# the policy file twpol.txt
# tripwire --check --email-report

exit

/* -------------------------------------
     /home/xcapncrunchx/tripwire.shBAK
-------------------------------------- */
#!/bin/sh
HOST_NAME=aestudio
TWHOME = /var/lib/tripwire
if [ ! -e $TWHOME/${HOST_NAME}.twd ]  ; then
echo "***Error: Tripwire DB for $[HOST_NAME] not found***."
echo "***Run 'tripwire --init'***"
else
test -f /etc/tripwire/tw.cfg && /usr/sbin/tripwire --check
fi

exit
##
# If you prefer your logs in the mail inbox, and not showed on screen,
configure this file, substitute
# the line beginning with 'test' by:
# test -f /etc/tripwire/tw.cfg && \ /usr/sbin/tripwire --check--email-
report \ --no-tty-output --silent
#

/* --------------------------------
     /home/xcapncrunchx/x1..x2.pub
---------------------------------- */
ssh-dss
AAAAB3NzaC1kc3MAAACBAIfTYcTaJWr/+UiQGO/PRGMmKSXcSg
gxWqttvl0qUIQAiHF4RFU7m1o2pqjA76SANh15bRRD+CPb484QstA35
PM4giR/ZsAif70fE1rfPTkKYICgabnNIB/ELvyUOfQ/umbBovGo+Eu
QPPovJw6hPP1sX1on+l5/Mr7tDNA+PsJBAAAAFQDQGBNt8rLSstA3
5PM4giR/ZsAif70fE1rfPTkKYICgabnNIB/ELvyUOfQ/umbBovGo+Eu
```

QPPovJw6hPP1sX1on+l5/Mr7tDNA+PsJBAAAAFQDQGBNt8rLS
stA35PM4giR/ZsAif70fE1rfPTkKYICgabnNIB/ELvyUOfQ/umbBovGo
+EuQPPovJw6hPP1sX1on+l5/Mr7tDNA+PsJBAAAAFQDQGBNt8rLS
stA35PM4giR/ZsAif70fE1rfPTkKYICgabnNIB/ELvyUOfQ/umbBovGo
+EuQPPovJw6hPP1sX1on+l5/Mr7tDNA+PsJBAAAAFQDQGBNt8rLS
H5TPxBWG2L/K2NMjbL8nv5AhpHZ62H0nAHfafqjZ9Zy3AI8=
xcapncrunchx@x1

```
/* --------------------------
        /home/xcapncrunchx/x1
-------------------------- */
```
        Nota: Este archivo es realmente un enlace simbólico a /etc/init.d/ssh-to.
```
#!/bin/sh
pass="PLAIN-ROOT_PASS-HERE-PLS"
sshpass -p "$pass" ssh `basename $0` $*
```

```
/* ------------------------------
        /home/xcapncrunchx/ssh-to
------------------------------- */
```
```
#!/bin/sh
pass="PLAIN-ROOT_PASS-HERE-PLS"
sshpass -p "$pass" ssh `basename $0` $*
```

```
/* ----------------------------------------------
        /home/xcapncrunchx/apache-logs-replication.sh
---------------------------------------------- */
```
```
!#/bin/sh
# Script to update 1 file like configuration file under /etc/ on many hosts
# at once. Add a row per host you want to update to (remote destiny).
# BEFORE RUN THE SCRIPT Ensure you that:
# 1. You run the script from the host which has the latest copy of the file
# you are synchronizing from (source)
# 2. The lines for hosts not to update were commented out or have been removed
# include the localhost.
# 3. Verify the file permissions are the correct before and after the propagation.
# Note: use rsync (update) or scp (overwrite) to make the tunnel to send the
# file update through it.
# Include restart/reload services or reboot commands if it is required.
pass="PLAIN-ROOT_PASS-HERE-PLS"
```

```
rsync -avv --rsh="sshpass -p $pass ssh" /var/log/apache2/
x1:/var/log/apache2/
#rsync -avv --rsh="sshpass -p $pass ssh" /etc/init.d/bastion-server-
firewall.sh x1:/etc/init.d/bastion-server-firewall.sh
#rsync -avv --rsh="sshpass -p $pass ssh" /etc/init.d/bastion-server-
firewall.sh x2:/etc/init.d/bastion-server-firewall.sh
#rsync -avv --rsh="sshpass -p $pass ssh" /etc/init.d/bastion-server-
firewall.sh x3:/etc/init.d/bastion-server-firewall.sh
#rsync -avv --rsh="sshpass -p $pass ssh" /etc/init.d/bastion-server-
firewall.sh x3:/etc/init.d/bastion-server-firewall.sh
#rsync -avv --rsh="sshpass -p $pass ssh" /etc/init.d/bastion-server-
firewall.sh y1:/etc/init.d/bastion-server-firewall.sh
#rsync -avv --rsh="sshpass -p $pass ssh" /etc/init.d/bastion-server-
firewall.sh y2:/etc/init.d/bastion-server-firewall.sh


/* ---------------------------------------------------------
      /home/xcapncrunchx/config-file-propagator-example.sh
--------------------------------------------------------- */
!#/bin/sh
# Script to update 1 file like configuration file under /etc/ on many hosts
# at once. Add a row per host you want to update to (remote destiny).
# BEFORE RUN THE SCRIPT Ensure you that:
# 1. You run the script from the host which has the latest copy of the file
# you are synchronizing from (source)
# 2. The lines for hosts not to update were commented out or have been
removed
# include the localhost.
# 3. Verify the file permissions are the correct before and after the
propagation.
# Note: use rsync (update) or scp (overwrite) to make the tunnel to send
the
# file update through it.
# Include restart/reload services or reboot commands if it is required.
pass="ROOT-PASS_HERE"
#rsync -avv --rsh="sshpass -p $pass ssh" /etc/init.d/bastion-server-
firewall.sh x1:/etc/init.d/bastion-server-firewall.sh
rsync -avv --rsh="sshpass -p $pass ssh" /home/xcapncrunchx/config-file-
update-propagation-template.sh       x1:/home/xcapncrunchx/config-file-
update-propagation-template.sh
#rsync -avv --rsh="sshpass -p $pass ssh" /etc/init.d/bastion-server-
firewall.sh x3:/etc/init.d/bastion-server-firewall.sh
#rsync -avv --rsh="sshpass -p $pass ssh" /etc/init.d/bastion-server-
firewall.sh x3:/etc/init.d/bastion-server-firewall.sh
```

```
#rsync -avv --rsh="sshpass -p $pass ssh" /etc/init.d/bastion-server-
firewall.sh y1:/etc/init.d/bastion-server-firewall.sh
#rsync -avv --rsh="sshpass -p $pass ssh" /etc/init.d/bastion-server-
firewall.sh y2:/etc/init.d/bastion-server-firewall.sh
```

```
/* ------------------------------------------------------------------
        /home/xcapncrunchx/config-file-update-propagation-template.sh
------------------------------------------------------------------ */
!#/bin/sh
# Script to update 1 file like configuration file under /etc/ on many hosts
# at once. Add a row per host you want to update to (remote destiny).
# BEFORE RUN THE SCRIPT Ensure you that:
# 1. You run the script from the host which has the latest copy of the file
# you are synchronizing from (source)
# 2. The lines for hosts not to update were commented out or have been
removed
# include the localhost.
# 3. Verify the file permissions are the correct before and after the
propagation.
# Note: use rsync (update) or scp (overwrite) to make the tunnel to send
the
# file update through it.
# Include restart/reload services or reboot commands if it is required.
pass="ROOT-PASS_HERE"
#rsync -avv --rsh="sshpass -p $pass ssh" /etc/init.d/bastion-server-
firewall.sh x1:/etc/init.d/bastion-server-firewall.sh
rsync -avv --rsh="sshpass -p $pass ssh" /etc/init.d/bastion-server-
firewall.sh x2:/etc/init.d/bastion-server-firewall.sh
#rsync -avv --rsh="sshpass -p $pass ssh" /etc/init.d/bastion-server-
firewall.sh x3:/etc/init.d/bastion-server-firewall.sh
#rsync -avv --rsh="sshpass -p $pass ssh" /etc/init.d/bastion-server-
firewall.sh x3:/etc/init.d/bastion-server-firewall.sh
#rsync -avv --rsh="sshpass -p $pass ssh" /etc/init.d/bastion-server-
firewall.sh y1:/etc/init.d/bastion-server-firewall.sh
#rsync -avv --rsh="sshpass -p $pass ssh" /etc/init.d/bastion-server-
firewall.sh y2:/etc/init.d/bastion-server-firewall.sh
```

```
/* ------------------------------------
        /home/xcapncrunchx/mail-purge.sh
-------------------------------------- */
#!/bin/sh
# Purges from the virtual mail boxes behind /var/vmail dir, the deleted
# mail, but not purged by users. Set this parameter in the option
```

\# '-ctime +7 ', taht tells the deleted mail of the last 7 days is going to
\# be completely deleted from the mail filesytem (local or remote,
\# ,E.G remotely using NFS).

find /var/vmail/ -type f -ctime +7 -name '*,ST' -print0 | xargs -r -0 rm -f

exit

```
* ------------------------------------
      /home/xcapncrunchx/webalizer.sh
------------------------------------- */
#!/bin/sh
# Updates the web sites visitors stats for webalizer, based in the site
# log file in /var/log/apache2/site-name.
# This file have to be added to a cron job in the crontab or pasted in the
# directory /etc/cron.hourly.

# Adds to the /home/user-name/tmp/webalizer/ dir the updated static
stats info.
# For every hosting site (user) listed. Check users against the correspondent
# apache "default" site's file.

# domain: aestudio.sytes.net
cd /home/aestudio/tmp/webalizer
/usr/bin/webalizer -q

# domain: cronos.sytes.net
#cd /home/web2/tmp/webalizer
#/usr/bin/webalizer -q

# domain: etribe.sytes.net
cd /home/etribe/tmp/webalizer
/usr/bin/webalizer -q

# domain: hereisthedeal.hopto.org
cd /home/hereisthedeal/tmp/webalizer
/usr/bin/webalizer –q

exit
```

4 VIDEO PROGRAMAS EN DVD

Todos los enlaces de descarga de los video programas que conforman Linux Enterprise Sci-Fi y de ser el caso y a criterio del Autor, Actualizaciones del Proyecto, Recursos Adicionales Externos y Errata, se encuentran disponibles en la siguiente dirección URL:
https://mega.co.nz/#F!IxcBnR7Q!NQKe67BdPtviVSNoZ4Vpcw

ACERCA DEL AUTOR

Esteban Herrera, Premio Nacional en Cine, antiguamente Actor y Comunicador y actualmente Consultor en Informática. Ha prestado servicios a algunos de los medios de comunicación más importantes de Costa Rica, como Radio Nacional, Radio Universidad de Costa Rica y el Diario La Nación.